# The ESL Teacher's BOOK OF LISTS

## Jacqueline E. Kress, Ed.D.

JOSSEY-BASS
A Wiley Imprint
www.josseybass.com

Published by Jossey-Bass
A Wiley Imprint
989 Market Street, San Francisco, CA 94103-1741    www.josseybass.com

Jossey-Bass books and products are available through most bookstores. To contact Jossey-Bass
directly call our Customer Care Department within the U.S. at (800) 956-7739, outside the U.S.
at (317) 572-3986 or fax (317) 572-4002.

Jossey-Bass also publishes its books in a variety of electronic formats. Some content that appears
in print may not be available in electronic books.

**Library of Congress Cataloging-in-Publication Data:**
Kress, Jacqueline E.
    The ESL teacher's book of lists / Jacqueline E. Kress.
        p.   cm.
    Includes bibliographical references.
    ISBN 0-7879-6738-6
    1. English language—study and teaching—Foreign speakers.
    2. Lists. I. Title
    PE1128.A2K74   1993                        93-2982
    428'.007—dc20

Printed in the United States of America
*PB Printing* 10  9  8  7  6  5

# About the Author

JACQUELINE E. KRESS, Ed.D., is an experienced teacher, teacher-trainer, educational program designer, and administrator. Her research in reading comprehension strategies earned her the 1987 Evelyn Headley Award from Rutgers University, where she earned her doctorate in reading. She has taught developmental and remedial reading and language arts in urban elementary schools as well as in several New Jersey colleges. She also served as a coordinator of elementary school reading and testing and as a college reading faculty member.

Dr. Kress has designed numerous educational programs for at-risk students with special instructional needs, including gifted and talented, underprepared, learning disabled, and visually or auditorily impaired students. She is the co- author of The Reading Teacher's Book of Lists (Prentice Hall, 3rd edition 1993) and The Readability Machine (Prentice Hall, 1986). Currently, Dr. Kress directs the Office of Total Quality Management at the New Jersey Department of Higher Education.

# About This Resource

*The ESL Teacher's Book of Lists* places in your hands eighty practical, classroom-tested lists you can reproduce for student use or refer to for help in planning highly effective lessons and activities. You will find a bounty of information and activities here, whether your students are brand new to English or are already mainstreamed into regular classes.

The seven sections of this resource cover all the bases: vocabulary, grammar, usage, pronunciation, assessment, and curriculum and instruction. Lists in the first three sections have been set up to be photocopied as necessary for use in the classroom. The lists in the last four sections can also be photocopied, but were primarily written to provide you with a ready fund of reference information, examples, and classroom techniques.

Section 1, *General Vocabulary*, provides twenty-one lists of English words students will need to use in various situations in daily life, ranging from "The 500 Most Frequently Used English Words" to lists for health, time, weather, money, travel, and more. Some of the most appealing lists in this section include an extensive section of American idioms, a list of idioms across five languages (English, Spanish, French, German, and Chinese), and three "shortcut" lists of cognates English shares with Spanish, French, and German, respectively.

Section 2, *Academic Vocabulary*, helps students get up to speed in the content areas, with one general school list and six basic and intermediate/advanced lists for mathematics, social studies, and science.

Section 3, *Grammar*, covers the basics of English grammar in thirteen quick, reproducible handouts with examples for students. In addition to the parts of speech you'll find the basic rules of punctuation, capitalization, spelling, and more.

Section 4, *Grammar Patterns and Practice*, provides nine complete lists you can draw on for classroom examples or drills, including various sentence patterns, subject/verb and time agreement, and common grammatical errors.

Section 5, *Pronunciation*, offers thirteen lists and charts you can use to help students learn to distinguish and make English sounds (including those most likely to cause problems for speakers of other languages) and practice English stress and intonation patterns in both words and sentences.

In Section 6, *Assessment*, you'll find seven comprehensive lists of techniques for assessing students' language proficiency, their auditory, aural, reading comprehension, oral language, and written language skills. There's also a list of commercial language tests.

Section 7, *Curriculum and Instruction*, brims over with practical teaching techniques and activities in ten lists you'll want to refer to again and again. Lists include suggestions for "Thematic Language Units," activities for improving auditory, aural, oral, vocabulary, grammar, and writing skills; selected instructional materials; and associations and resource centers for ESL teachers.

Finally, you'll find a complete glossary of terms used in the book, an indispensable guide to the specialized language of ESL instruction.

Whether you teach in a self-contained ESL classroom, teach ESL students who also attend regular classes, or want to help ESL students who have been mainstreamed into your reading or English classroom, you'll find yourself returning again and again to *The ESL Teacher's Book of Lists* for ready-to-use information and ideas!

*Jacqueline E. Kress, Ed.D.*

# Contents

## SECTION 3.  GRAMMAR • 65

## SECTION 4.  GRAMMAR PATTERNS AND PRACTICE • 103

## SECTION 5.  PRONUNCIATION • 127

# SECTION 6.   ASSESSMENT • 161

# SECTION 7.   CURRICULUM AND INSTRUCTION • 183

# SECTION 1
# General Vocabulary

# 1-1  TOP OF THE CHART:
## The 500 Most Frequently Used English Words
## (in ranked order)

**1-25**

| | | | | |
|---|---|---|---|---|
| the | in | he | as | at |
| of | is | was | with | be |
| and | you | for | his | this |
| a | that | on | they | have |
| to | it | are | I | from |

**26-50**

| | | | | |
|---|---|---|---|---|
| or | but | we | there | she |
| one | not | when | use | do |
| had | what | your | an | how |
| by | all | can | each | their |
| word | were | said | which | if |

**51-75**

| | | | | |
|---|---|---|---|---|
| will | many | some | him | two |
| up | then | her | into | more |
| other | them | would | time | write |
| about | these | make | has | go |
| out | so | like | look | see |

**76-100**

| | | | | |
|---|---|---|---|---|
| number | my | call | find | get |
| no | than | who | long | come |
| way | first | oil | down | made |
| could | water | its | day | may |
| people | been | now | did | part |

**101-125**

| | | | | |
|---|---|---|---|---|
| over | little | live | very | name |
| new | work | me | after | good |
| sound | know | back | thing | sentence |
| take | place | give | our | man |
| only | year | most | just | think |

**126-150**

| | | | | |
|---|---|---|---|---|
| say | much | mean | boy | also |
| great | before | old | follow | around |

## 126-150 (*continued*)

| | | | | |
|---|---|---|---|---|
| where | line | any | came | form |
| help | right | same | want | three |
| through | too | tell | show | small |

## 151-175

| | | | | |
|---|---|---|---|---|
| set | well | such | ask | land |
| put | large | because | went | different |
| end | must | turn | men | home |
| does | big | here | read | us |
| another | even | why | need | move |

## 176-200

| | | | | |
|---|---|---|---|---|
| try | change | away | letter | still |
| kind | off | animal | mother | learn |
| hand | play | house | answer | should |
| picture | spell | point | found | American |
| again | air | page | study | world |

## 201-225

| | | | | |
|---|---|---|---|---|
| high | between | last | never | light |
| every | own | school | start | thought |
| near | below | father | city | head |
| add | country | keep | earth | under |
| food | plant | tree | eye | story |

## 226-250

| | | | | |
|---|---|---|---|---|
| saw | along | next | life | together |
| left | might | hard | always | got |
| don't | close | open | those | group |
| few | something | example | both | often |
| while | seem | begin | paper | run |

## 251-275

| | | | | |
|---|---|---|---|---|
| important | car | sea | four | hear |
| until | mile | began | carry | stop |
| children | night | grow | state | without |
| side | walk | took | once | second |
| feet | white | river | book | later |

## 276-300

| | | | | |
|---|---|---|---|---|
| miss | watch | let | cut | song |
| idea | far | above | young | being |
| enough | Indian | girl | talk | leave |
| eat | real | sometimes | soon | family |
| face | almost | mountain | list | it's |

**301-325**

| | | | | |
|---|---|---|---|---|
| body | questions | horse | knew | usually |
| music | fish | birds | since | didn't |
| color | area | problem | ever | friends |
| stand | mark | complete | piece | easy |
| sun | dog | room | told | heard |

**326-350**

| | | | | |
|---|---|---|---|---|
| order | top | short | hours | measure |
| red | ship | better | black | remember |
| door | across | best | products | early |
| sure | today | however | happened | waves |
| become | during | low | whole | reached |

**351-375**

| | | | | |
|---|---|---|---|---|
| listen | fast | five | true | table |
| wind | several | step | hundred | north |
| rock | hold | morning | against | slowly |
| space | himself | passed | pattern | money |
| covered | toward | vowel | numeral | map |

**376-400**

| | | | | |
|---|---|---|---|---|
| farm | cold | sing | town | field |
| pulled | cried | war | I'll | travel |
| draw | plan | ground | unit | wood |
| voice | notice | fall | figure | fire |
| seen | south | king | certain | upon |

**401-425**

| | | | | |
|---|---|---|---|---|
| done | fly | correct | shown | front |
| English | gave | oh | minutes | feel |
| road | box | quickly | strong | fact |
| half | finally | person | verb | inches |
| ten | wait | became | stars | street |

**426-450**

| | | | | |
|---|---|---|---|---|
| decided | building | rest | stay | less |
| contain | ocean | carefully | green | machine |
| course | class | scientists | known | base |
| surface | note | inside | island | ago |
| produce | nothing | wheels | week | stood |

**451-475**

| | | | | |
|---|---|---|---|---|
| plane | boat | warm | though | yes |
| system | game | common | language | clear |
| behind | force | bring | shape | equation |

## 451-475 (*continued*)

| ran | brought | explain | deep | yet |
| round | understand | dry | thousands | government |

## 476-500

| filled | object | power | dark | fine |
| heat | am | cannot | ball | pair |
| full | rule | able | material | circle |
| hot | among | six | special | include |
| check | noun | size | heavy | built |

# 1-2 BE CAREFUL:
## Safety Words

accident
alarm
ambulance
break glass
burn
caution
combustible
cop
crash
danger
do not cross
do not drink
do not enter
doctor
don't walk
down

drinking water
drugs
emergency
entrance
exit
explosion
explosive
fire
fire exit
fire extinguisher
fireman
first aid
flammable
gas
guard
handle with care

harmful if swallowed
hospital
keep out
no admittance
no smoking
no trespassing
poison
police
policeman
robbery
security office
security officer
up
walk
warning

**Common Idioms**

to be assaulted          to be mugged          to lose ———

to be hurt               to be robbed          to need a policeman

to be in an accident     to fall               to need an ambulance

to be injured            to go for help        to need help

to be lost               to look for           to stay calm

*to be assaulted*

# 1-3  FILL IN THE BLANKS:
## Words on Applications and Forms

accepted
account
address
advisor
agency
alien
alien registration card
allowance
amount
annual
applicant
application
assistance
attached
authorized
available
balance
bank account
baptismal certificate
beneficiary
benefits
birth certificate
blank
Blue Cross
Blue Shield
cancelled check
car

certificate
check
check the box
checking account
city
claim
college
company
complete
consent
counselor
country of origin
credit
credit card
credit check
creditors
date
date of birth
day
deduction
department
dependent
deposit
disability
divorced
dotted line
driver's license

each
education
elementary
school
eligible
employer
employment
enrolled
ethnic group
ethnicity
ever
exempt
felony
fill in
fill out
first
first name
grade
green card
health insurance
high school
HMO
home address
homeowner
immigrant
immigration
office

impairment
income
income tax return
independent
insurance
insurance card
interest rate
landlady
landlord
last name
lease
license
list
mailing address
marital status
married
matriculated
military
money order
monthly
mortgage
nationality
next of kin
non-relative
notarized
notary public
passbook
passport

permit
personnel
phone number
physician
policy
post office box
previous
print
proficiency test
qualifications
race
receipt
referred
registration
relative
religion
renewal
rent
requirements
resources
revoked
schedule
school records
secondary school
section
separated
service charge
sign

signature
single
social security
  number
spouse
state
statement
student
student visa
surname
tax
temporary
tenant
total
town
transcript
type
university
utilities
valid
vehicle
  registration
withdrawal
witness
write
year
ZIP Code
zone

# 1–4 FEELING WELL?:
## Health Words

**External Parts of the Body**

abdomen
Adam's apple
ankle(s)
arm(s)
back
breast(s)
buttocks
calf (calves)
cheek(s)
chest
chin
collarbone
dimple(s)
ear lobe(s)
ear(s)
elbow(s)
eye(s)
eyebrow(s)
eyelash(es)
eyelid(s)
face
finger(s)
fingernail(s)
fist(s)

foot (feet)
forearm(s)
forehead
genitals
hair
hand(s)
head
heel(s)
hip(s)
jaw
knee(s)
kneecap(s)
leg(s)
lip(s)
mouth
neck
nose
palm(s)
penis
rectum
rib(s)
shin(s)
shoulder(s)
sole(s)

spine
stomach
temple(s)
testicles
thigh(s)
throat
thumb(s)
toe(s)
tongue
tooth (teeth)
vagina
waist
wrist(s)

*The ESL Teacher's Book of Lists,* © 1993 by John Wiley & Sons, Inc.

**Internal Parts of the Body**

appendix
bladder
blood
bone(s)
brain

heart
intestines
kidney(s)
liver
lung(s)

muscle(s)
nerve(s)
tonsils
vein(s)

**Complaints**

accident
ache
allergic
have an allergy
bleeding
burn
chest pains
chills

constipation
cramps
cut
diarrhea
dizzy
feel faint
fever
head cold

headache
hurt
injury
nausea
pain
rash
runny nose
sore

11

## Complaints (*continued*)

| | | |
|---|---|---|
| sore throat | tender | wound |
| stiffness | vomiting | ace bandage |
| swollen | | |

## Diagnoses and Doctor's Orders

| | | |
|---|---|---|
| anesthesia | German measles | liquid |
| antibiotics | heal | measles |
| aspirin | heart attack | medication |
| asthma | heating pad | medicine |
| Band-Aid® | hepatitis | mono |
| bandage | high blood pressure | mononucleosis |
| bed rest | ice pack | mumps |
| birth control | | operation |
| blind | | oxygen |
| blister | | period |
| blood test | | pills |
| broken | | pneumonia |
| bronchitis | | pregnant |
| cancer | | prescription |
| cast | | pulse |
| chicken pox | | recuperate |
| coma | | rest |
| concussion | | rubella |
| condom | | sanitary |
| contraceptive | | napkins |
| cough syrup | | scrape |
| crutches | | shot |
| deaf | | soak |
| decongestant | | sprain |
| diabetes | | stitches |
| diet | | stroke |
| dislocated | | surgery |
| drugs | infected | tablet |
| examination | infection | tampon |
| examine | inflammation | ulcer |
| flu | injection | urine analysis |
| fracture | insulin | virus |
| gargle | lab tests | vitamins |
| gauze | laxative | X-ray |

## People

| | | |
|---|---|---|
| doctor | optician | physician |
| eye doctor | optometrist | psychiatrist |
| gynecologist | patient | psychologist |
| lab technician | pediatrician | specialist |
| nurse | pharmacist | surgeon |

*The ESL Teacher's Book of Lists*, © 1993 by John Wiley & Sons, Inc.

## Places and Things

ambulance
cardiac care unit
clinic
delivery room
drug store
emergency room
examination room

hospital
injection
insurance card
insurance form
intensive care unit
labor room
laboratory

needle
pharmacy
thermometer
treatment room
waiting room

## Dental Health

bite
braces
cavity
check-up
chin
cleaning
dentures
drill
false teeth
filling
floss
gargle
gums
jaw
molar
mouthwash
nerve
Novocaine
plaque
root canal
toothache
toothbrush
toothpaste
wisdom tooth
X-ray

## Basic Phrases

How are you?
I'm fine.
I don't feel well.
I'm sick.
I feel dizzy.
I need a doctor.
Call an ambulance.
Take me to a hospital.

**Basic Phrases (*continued*)**

Where's the nurse's office?

Where's the doctor's office?

This is an emergency.

Take two of these pills every four hours.

I have a cold.

I have a sore throat.

I have a backache.

I have a cough.

I have a fever.

I have a headache.

I have something in my eye.

I sprained my ankle.

My arm hurts. (My arms hurt.)

My leg hurts. (My legs hurt.)

# 1–5  RELATIVELY SPEAKING: Family Words

| Female | Male |
|---|---|
| wife | husband |
| mother | father |
| mom | dad |
| mommy | daddy |
| sister | brother |
| daughter | son |
| aunt | uncle |
| grandmother | grandfather |
| grandma | grandpa |
| granddaughter | grandson |
| niece | nephew |
| cousin | cousin |
| step-mother | step-father |
| foster mother | foster father |
| half-sister | half-brother |
| mother-in-law | father-in-law |
| sister-in-law | brother-in-law |
| great-aunt | great-uncle |
| great-grandmother | great-grandfather |
| godmother | godfather |
| widow | widower |
| maternal relatives | paternal relatives |
| ma | pa |
| mom | pop |

## General

| | |
|---|---|
| family | spouse |
| relatives | adopted |
| relations | adoptive |
| next of kin | grandchild |
| parents | grandchildren |
| children | baby |
| siblings | infant |
| guardian | child |
| orphan | toddler |
| divorcee | teenager |
| folks | twins |
| dependent | triplets |

# 1–6 *YOU CAN COUNT ON IT:* *Numbers*

| 0 | zero | | |
|---|------|---|---|
| 1 | one | 1st | first |
| 2 | two | 2nd | second |
| 3 | three | 3rd | third |
| 4 | four | 4th | fourth |
| 5 | five | 5th | fifth |
| 6 | six | 6th | sixth |
| 7 | seven | 7th | seventh |
| 8 | eight | 8th | eighth |
| 9 | nine | 9th | ninth |
| 10 | ten | 10th | tenth |
| 11 | eleven | 11th | eleventh |
| 12 | twelve | 12th | twelfth |
| 13 | thirteen | 13th | thirteenth |
| 14 | fourteen | 14th | fourteenth |
| 15 | fifteen | 15th | fifteenth |
| 16 | sixteen | 16th | sixteenth |
| 17 | seventeen | 17th | seventeenth |
| 18 | eighteen | 18th | eighteenth |
| 19 | nineteen | 19th | nineteenth |
| 20 | twenty | 20th | twentieth |
| 21 | twenty-one | 21st | twenty-first |
| 22 | twenty-two | 22nd | twenty-second |
| 23 | twenty-three | 23rd | twenty-third |

*The ESL Teacher's Book of Lists,* © 1993 by John Wiley & Sons, Inc.

| | | | |
|---|---|---|---|
| 24 | twenty-four | 24th | twenty-fourth |
| 25 | twenty-five | 25th | twenty-fifth |
| 30 | thirty | 30th | thirtieth |
| 31 | thirty-one | 31st | thirty-first |
| 40 | forty | 40th | fortieth |
| 41 | forty-one | 41st | forty-first |
| 50 | fifty | 50th | fiftieth |
| 60 | sixty | 60th | sixtieth |
| 70 | seventy | 70th | seventieth |
| 80 | eighty | 80th | eightieth |
| 90 | ninety | 90th | ninetieth |
| 100 | one hundred | 100th | one hundreth |
| 150 | one hundred fifty | | |
| 200 | two hundred | | |
| 500 | five hundred | | |
| 1,000 | one thousand | | |
| 1,100 | one thousand one hundred | | |
| 1,100 | eleven hundred | | |
| 1,500 | one thousand five hundred | | |
| 1,500 | fifteen hundred | | |
| 2,000 | two thousand | | |
| 1,000,000 | one million | | one millionth |
| 1,000,000,000 | one billion | | one billionth |

# 1-7 *WAITING FOR THE WEEKEND: Calendar Words*

**Days of the Week**

| | |
|---|---|
| Monday | Mon. |
| Tuesday | Tues. |
| Wednesday | Wed. |
| Thursday | Thurs. |
| Friday | Fri. |
| Saturday | Sat. |
| Sunday | Sun. |

**Months**

| | |
|---|---|
| January | Jan. |
| February | Feb. |
| March | Mar. |
| April | Apr. |
| May | May |
| June | Jun. |
| July | Jul. |
| August | Aug. |
| September | Sept. |
| October | Oct. |
| November | Nov. |
| December | Dec. |

*The ESL Teacher's Book of Lists,* © 1993 by John Wiley & Sons, Inc.

**Major Holidays**

| | |
|---|---|
| New Year's Day | January 1 |
| Martin Luther King, Jr., Day | January 15 |
| Groundhog Day | February 2 |
| Lincoln's Birthday | February 12 |
| Valentine's Day | February 14 |
| Washington's Birthday | February 22 |
| St. Patrick's Day | March 17 |
| April Fool's Day | April 1 |
| Mother's Day | 2nd Sunday of May |
| Memorial Day | last Monday of May |
| Father's Day | 3rd Sunday of June |
| Independence Day | July 4 |
| Labor Day | 1st Monday of September |
| Columbus Day | October 12 |
| Halloween | October 31 |
| Veteran's Day | November 11 |
| Thanksgiving Day | 4th Thursday of November |
| Christmas Day | December 25 |
| New Year's Eve | December 31 |

November 20, 1993          11/20/93
11-20-93                   Nov. 20, 1993
date                       week
weekday                    weekend
holiday                    season
vacation                   semester break

# 1–8 GOT A MINUTE?:
## Time Words

What time is it?

It is one o'clock.

It's 1 A.M. (in the morning)

It's 1 P.M. (in the afternoon)

It's 1:30 P.M.

It's noon.

It's twelve o'clock.

It's midnight.

| | | |
|---|---|---|
| It's a quarter to nine. | It's 8:45. | It's eight forty-five. |
| It's a quarter after nine. | It's 9:15. | It's nine fifteen. |
| It's half past six. | It's 6:30. | It's six thirty. |
| It's five of seven. | It's 6:55. | It's six fifty-five. |
| It's around seven. | It's about seven. | |
| It's ten after eight. | It's 8:10. | It's eight ten. |

A.M. (after midnight, but before noon)

P.M. (after noon, but before midnight)

to tell time

to set the clock

to set the watch

to synchronize your watches

to wind your watch

to beat the clock

to punch in

sunrise

dawn

sun-up

daybreak

morning

daytime

| | | |
|---|---|---|
| daylight | minute | weekly |
| noon | quarter hour | monthly |
| midday | half hour | annually |
| afternoon | hour | yearly |
| sunset | day | clock |
| sundown | week | watch |
| dusk | month | wristwatch |
| twilight | year | calendar |
| evening | leap year | stopwatch |
| night | decade | timer |
| midnight | century | clock radio |
| second | daily | alarm clock |

# 1-9 ON A CLEAR DAY:
## Weather Words

### Adjectives

arctic

balmy

breezy

brisk

calm

chilly

clear

clearing

cloudy

cold

cool

damp

dreary

dry

foggy

freezing

frigid

hazy

hot

humid

icy

mild

misty

overcast

snowy

sunny

sweltering

tropical

warm

wet

windy

### Nouns

barometer

blizzard

climate

clouds

cyclone

degrees

dew

downpour

drizzle

fog

frost

gale

gust

hail

hailstones

heat wave

humidity

hurricane

ice

lightning

precipitation

rain

raindrops

shower

sleet

snow

snowdrifts

snowflakes

snowstorm

squall

sunshine

temperature

thunder

thunderstorm

tornado

tropical storm

weather

weather forecast

weather report

weather vane

wind

# 1–10 LET'S GO:
## Transportation and Travel Words

airplane
airport
airsick
arrivals
auto
baggage
baggage claim
bike
birth certificate
boarding pass
bridge
bus
bus driver
bus station
bus stop
cabin attendant
captain
car
car keys
check in/out
claim ticket
conductor
connection
crosswalk
curve
dead battery
dead end
departures
detour
divided highway
do not enter
do not pass
driver's license
driver's permit
east
elevator
entrance
exit
ferry
fire hydrant
flat tire
freeway
gas

gasoline
gas station
gate
guest(s)
helicopter
hotel
identification
inn
insurance
intersection
interstate
itinerary
junction
keep right
left lane ends
life jacket
luggage
merge
motel
no left turn
no right turn
no turns
north
observation deck
oil
one way

parking lot
parking meter
parkway
passport
pilot
plane
reduce speed
register
registration
reservation
restaurant
restroom
right lane ends
route
schedule
service station
ship
sign (advertisement)
slow
south
speed limit
stop
subway
thruway
ticket
tire

token

toll

toll booth

towaway zone

traffic

traffic jam

train

train station

travel agent

trunk (of a car)

turnpike

use alternate route

vehicle

visa

west

wheel

winding road

window

wrong way

yield

### Common Idioms

to back up the car

to board

to buy a ticket

to call a cab

to circle

to crash

to fasten the seat belt

to get a parking ticket

to get in the car

to get on

to go through customs

to go through security

to hail a taxi

to have an accident

to land

to park the car

to pick up one's baggage

to speed

to start the car

to take off

## 1–11 *I'M PLEASED TO MEET YOU:*
### *Social Words*

Hello.

Good morning.

How are you doing?

Fine, thanks.

What's your name?

My name is _____.

Where do you live?

I live on _____ Street.

What's your address?

I'm at 14 Timber Lane, High City.

My address is 615 Second Street,
Riverdale.

Where do you go to school?

What classes do you have this year?

When did you move here?

Where did you live before?

What grade are you in?

I'm in _____ grade. (first, second,...
eighth)

I'm a freshman. (sophomore, junior,
senior)

Are you new here?

Where's the cafeteria?

Where's the library?

Where's the gym?

Is there a game tonight?

Do we have practice?

Do you like to dance?

Do you like music?

Would you like to go to the game?

I'm hungry.

Do you want to get some lunch?

Thanks.

Thank you.

Thanks a lot.

See you later.

See you tomorrow.

Call me tonight.

What's your phone number?

*The ESL Teacher's Book of Lists*, © 1993 by John Wiley & Sons, Inc.

Where are you going?

What's the matter?

Have a nice day.

Bye now.

Bye-bye.

So long.

Good night.

Excuse me.

I'm sorry.

Pardon me.

I apologize.

That's all right.

Go ahead.

Come on, let's go.

Come on in.

I've got to go now.

I appreciate it.

You're very kind.

No, thank you.

Yes, please.

May I help you?

Would you help me, please?

Of course.

No problem.

It would be a pleasure.

Who is that?

That's Robert.

Would you introduce us?

Jack, this is Robert.

Nice to meet you.

Please join us.

Thanks for calling.

Congratulations!

Happy Birthday!

What's that?

I don't know.

Who knows?

It's nothing.

# 1-12  RED, WHITE, AND —:
## Colors

| | |
|---|---|
| beige | off-white |
| black | olive green |
| blue | orange |
| bronze | peach |
| brown | pink |
| copper | plum |
| cream | purple |
| forest green | red |
| gold | rose |
| gray | silver |
| green | sky blue |
| ivory | tan |
| khaki | taupe |
| lavender | teal |
| lemon yellow | turquoise |
| magenta | violet |
| maroon | white |
| mint green | yellow |
| navy blue | |

*The ESL Teacher's Book of Lists,* © 1993 by John Wiley & Sons, Inc.

# 1–13  *A MILLION DOLLARS:*
## *Money Words*

| | | | | |
|---|---|---|---|---|
| $ | .01 | 1 cent | one penny | 1/100 of a dollar |
| $ | .02 | 2 cents | two pennies | 1/50 of a dollar |
| $ | .05 | 5 cents | one nickel | 1/20 of a dollar |
| $ | .10 | 10 cents | one dime | 1/10 of a dollar |
| $ | .25 | 25 cents | one quarter | 1/4 of a dollar |
| $ | .50 | 50 cents | one half-dollar | 1/2 of a dollar |
| $ | 1.00 | 100 cents | one dollar bill | 1 dollar |
| $ | 5.00 | | five-dollar bill | 5 dollars |
| $ | 10.00 | | ten-dollar bill | 10 dollars |
| $ | 20.00 | | twenty-dollar bill | 20 dollars |
| $ | 50.00 | | fifty-dollar bill | 50 dollars |
| $100.00 | | | one-hundred dollar bill | 100 dollars |

automated teller
  machine (ATM)
balance
bank
bank account
bills
cash
cash machine
change
charge
check
checking account
coin
cost
count
credit card
currency
deposit
discount

exchange rate
for sale
fortune
interest
investments
loan
millionaire
money
money order
on sale
paycheck
price
receipt
sales tax
savings account
sign
teller
tip
total

traveler's check
wealthy
withdrawal

## Common Idioms

to borrow
to bounce a check
to cash a check
to change a bill
to charge (a purchase or service;
  use a credit card)
to charge (a rate; cost)
to endorse a check
to get change

to get a loan
to lend
to make a deposit
to make a withdrawal
to put money in a bank
to save
to spend
to take money out of the bank
to use a cash machine

# 1-14  *CATCH MY DRIFT?:*
## *American Idioms*

It's about time you showed up.
You finally arrived.

He's afraid of his own shadow.
He's easily frightened.

We're working against the clock.
We haven't much time.

All systems go.
Everything is ready.

I'm all thumbs.
I'm clumsy.

It costs an arm and a leg.
It's very expensive.

He's asleep at the switch.
He's not paying attention.

She's at sixes and sevens.
She's not organized.

His back is to the wall.
He is trapped by the circumstances.

I'll take a baker's dozen.
I'll take thirteen.

Tom is a real ball of fire.
Tom is good and quick.

Stop beating around the bush.
Stop avoiding the issue.

Sal's behind the eight-ball.
Sal's in trouble.

Have you met my better half?
Have you met my spouse?

Carl's just biding his time.
Carl's just waiting for a chance.

The bank robber finally bit the dust.
The bank robber finally died.

It makes your blood run cold.
It's horrifying.

Ned is boning up on his German.
Ned is reviewing his German lessons.

The bottom line is NO!
The final answer is NO!

The show brought down the house.
The show was a great success.

Have you seen his bucket of bolts?
Have you seen his very old and worn car?

Don't burn the midnight oil.
Don't stay up too late.

I'm going to catch forty winks.
I'm going to take a nap.

Jill caught his eye.
Jill attracted his attention.

He had his wings clipped.
His activities were restricted.

Tara gave him the cold shoulder.
Tara ignored him.

The prisoner came clean.
The prisoner confessed.

Don't darken my door again.
Don't come back here again.

He was dead to the world.
He was in a deep sleep.

Bill is down in the dumps.
Bill is depressed.

Drop me a line soon.
Write me a letter soon.

He was the fair-haired boy.
He was the favorite.

Her feet are on the ground.
She is sensible.

No one can fill his shoes.
No one can replace him.

They flew the coop.
They disappeared.

Get off my back.
Stop bothering me.

Gail got the ax.
Gail was fired from her job.

I think I've got the feel of it.
I think I have learned to do it.

We just got wind of it.
We just heard about it.

Go fly a kite.
Go away.

*She was a feather of a girl.*
*She didn't weigh very much.*

John's a good egg.
John's a good person.

Mom's got a green thumb.
Mom's a successful gardener.

The girls are having a ball.
The girls are enjoying themselves.

I think he has a screw loose.
I think he's a little crazy.

Keep your head above water.
Stay out of trouble.

My heart goes out to her.
I feel sorry for her.

I have to hit the books tonight.
I have to study tonight.

I have a little hole-in-the-wall.
I have a small, inexpensive apartment.

Gene is always in a fog.
Gene is always confused.

Joe's in hot water.
Joe's in trouble.

It's still up in the air.
It's still undecided.

Just jump through the hoops.
Just do what you are told to do.

Keep your nose clean.
Stay out of trouble.

Keep the ball rolling.
Continue the activity.

I will leave no stone unturned.
I will try everything.

Let your hair down tonight.
Relax tonight.

He lost his shirt on that bet.
He lost a lot of money on that bet.

Let's make tracks.
Let's hurry.

It happens once in a blue moon.
It happens very seldom.

He's still on the fence.
He's still undecided.

Did he pop the question?
Did he ask you to marry him?

*The ESL Teacher's Book of Lists,* © 1993 by John Wiley & Sons, Inc.

I put two and two together.
I used the facts to make my decision.

By evening she was run ragged.
By evening she was very tired.

I see the light now.
I understand now.

We did it on a shoestring.
We did it with very little money.

Don't spread yourself thin.
Don't do many things at once.

You bet.
Certainly.

He took pains with his work.
He was very careful with his work.

The boys thumbed a ride home.
The boys hitchhiked home.

I'll do it when hell freezes over.
I'll never do it.

Can you lend me a hand?
Can you help me?

Stop beating about the bush.
Stop delaying.

Mr. Divens has a heart of gold.
Mr. Divens is kind and generous.

Give me a break, will you?
Stop bothering me.

He zonked out in the chair.
He fell asleep in the chair.

Cut it out, will you?
Stop doing that, will you?

It's raining cats and dogs.
It's raining very hard.

Tony doesn't have a prom date; Jill's in the same boat.
Tony doesn't have a prom date; Jill doesn't have one either.

Harry put his foot in his mouth.
Harry said something that made him appear foolish.

This letter belongs in the circular file.
This letter belongs in the trash.

His yellow hat made him stand out in the crowd.
He was easy to find in the crowd because of his yellow hat.

Please get in touch with me by Friday.
Please telephone or write to me by Friday.

Hang on and I'll ask my sister if she has the tickets.
Wait while I ask my sister if she has the tickets.

Don't give up now, you've almost got it.
Don't quit now, you've almost got it.

I'd give my right arm to know what he said.
I'd pay a large price to know what he said.

I never believed he'd turn his back on me like this.
I never believed he would leave me.

Karyn's new job was in the bag.
The arrangements for Karyn's new job were complete.

I was banking on getting that raise.
I believed I was getting that raise.

Carol spilled the beans about Arne's surprise party.
Carol told someone about Arne's surprise party.

I've been beating my brains out trying to find the answer.
I've worked hard to find the answer.

I don't know if he'll beat the rap or not.
I don't know if the court will find him innocent.

When Tommy was late, Anna was beside herself with fear.
When Tommy was late, Anna was extremely fearful.

Art surprised everyone when he made it big.
Art surprised everyone when he became a success.

I will never have another blind date!
I will never again agree to a date arranged by other people.

Cory missed the boat when he turned down the boss's offer.
Cory missed a good opportunity when he turned down the boss's offer.

Tom said he has a bone to pick with Penny.
Tom said he has a problem to resolve with Penny.

The President discussed the issue with his brain trust.
The President discussed the issue with his group of experts.

They found a bug in the mayor's phone.
They found a hidden listening device in the mayor's phone.

He turned his room upside down looking for his wallet.
He looked everywhere in his room for his wallet.

I think I'll just bum around the museum for an hour or so.
I think I'll wander around in the museum for an hour or so.

Bundle up, or you'll catch a cold.
Dress warmly, or you'll become ill.

I bumped into my old boyfriend at the game last night.
I met my former boyfriend at the game last night.

No one bought his excuse for being late again.
No one believed his excuse for being late again.

*The ESL Teacher's Book of Lists,* © 1993 by John Wiley & Sons, Inc.

I'm tired; I think I'll call it a day.
I'm tired; I think I'll stop working now.

It never crossed my mind that it was a fake diamond.
I did not think that it was a fake diamond.

I'm too shy; I don't think I'm cut out to be an actress.
I'm too shy; I don't think I have the right qualities to be an actress.

This car can stop on a dime.
This car can stop very quickly.

His constant singing can drive you to drink.
His constant singing can make you very nervous.

Ella was always on the edge.
Ella was always very nervous.

While she was sick, she fell behind her class in math.
While she was sick, she did not continue in math at the same pace as her classmates.

Taking drugs is playing with fire.
Taking drugs is very dangerous.

Mom will hit the ceiling when she sees this mess.
Mom will be very angry when she sees this mess.

It was hard to hold my tongue while I listened to the lies.
While I listened to the lies, I was very tempted to speak out against them.

He was put in a hospital because he lost his mind.
He was put in a hospital because he became insane.

Aspirin is an over-the-counter drug.
Aspirin can be purchased without a doctor's prescription.

Kim had taken great pains with the sign, and it looked great.
Kim had been very careful with the sign, and it looked great.

Nina passed a remark about Georgio's haircut.
Nina said something unkind about Georgio's haircut.

The man's mother passed away in April.
The man's mother died in April.

Ed's car was stolen, and he tried to pin it on Tony.
Ed's car was stolen, and he blamed Tony.

Steve decided he would pop the question on Rose's birthday.
Steve decided he would propose marriage on Rose's birthday.

If we put our heads together we could think of a good present.
If we work together, we could think of a good present.

She ran into her secretary at the library.
She unexpectedly met her secretary at the library.

Bob's father was in his second childhood.
Bob's father was old and returning to childish behavior.

*The ESL Teacher's Book of Lists,* © 1993 by John Wiley & Sons, Inc.

# 1–15  A FIVE-WAY TIE:
## Idioms Across Five Languages

| English | Spanish | French | German | Chinese |
|---|---|---|---|---|
| all right | bien | c'est bien | zufrieden sein | ānrán wúyàng |
| at once | enseguida | tout de suite | gleich | lìkè |
| be in the way | estorbar | être de trop | im Wege sein | fáng ài |
| big deal | gran cosa | grande chose | grosse Sache | míng-ren |
| call up | llamar | téléphoner | anrufen | dǎ diàn-huà |
| catch on | darse cuenta | y être | verstehen | líjiě |
| cross out | tachar | barrer | ausstreichen | huà héngxiàn chuānguò |
| do over | rehacer | refaire | wiederholen | zuò zài |
| dream up | soñar | rêver | aufdenken | píngkōng xiǎngchū |
| drop out | dejar de asistir | quitter | verlassen | tuìchū |
| figure out | razonar | calculer | herausfinden | líjiě |
| fill out | llenar | remplir | ausfüllen | biàndà |
| fool around | perder el tiempo | perdre son temps | Unsinn machen | yóudàng |
| get better | mejorar | aller mieux | besser werden | fùyuán |
| get off | apearse | descendre | aussteigen | xià |
| get on | montarse | monter | einsteigen | zài chuán shàng |
| get sick | enfermarse | tomber malade | krank werden | gǎn-mào |
| get up | levantarse | se lever | aufstehen | qǐlai |
| hand in | presentar | remettre | einreichen | yíjiāo |
| knock it off | dejar de | cesser imméd-iatemente | aufhören | tíngzhǐ |
| let go of | soltar | lâcher | freilassen | shìfàng |
| lie down | acostarse | s'étendre | sich hinlegen | tǎng-xià |
| look at | mirar | regarder | ansehen | kàn |
| look for | buscar | chercher | suchen | zhǎo |
| make believe | pretender | prétendre | vortauschen | jiǎzhuāng |
| make sense | ser lógico | être logique | verständig sein | yǒu yìyì |
| never mind | no importa | peu importe | schon gut | méiguānxi |
| on purpose | a proposito | exprès | absichtlich | gùyìde |
| on the whole | en general | en somme | im Allgemeinen | zòngde lài kàn |
| out of order | descompuesto | ne pas fonctionner | ausser Betrieb | chū cùzhàng |
| over and over | repetidamente | sans cesse | immer wieder | fǎnfù |
| pick out | seleccionar | choiser | aussuchen | tiāo |
| put away | guardar | ranger | weglegen | fànghǎo |
| put off | aplazar | remettre | aufschieben | tuīchí |
| put on | ponerse | mettre | aufsetzen | chuānshàng |
| right away | inmediatamente | immédiatement | sofort | mǎ-shàng |
| run errands | hacer mandados | faire des courses | Besorgungen machen | gàn chāshi |
| sit down | sentarse | s'asseoir | sich hinsetzen | zuòxià |
| stand up | ponerse de pie | se mettre debout | aufstehen | zhàn-qi-lái |

| English | Spanish | French | German | Chinese |
|---|---|---|---|---|
| take off | quitarse | enlever | ausziehen | qǐfēi |
| take over | encargarse de | se charger de | übernehmen | jiēren zhí wù |
| take turns | alternar | alterner | abwechseln | lúnliú zuò moùshì |
| talk over | discutir | discuter | beschprechen | shāng liàng |
| think over | pensar | réfléchir | überlegen | zìxì kǎolù |
| throw away | botar | jeter | wegwerfen | làngfèidiào |
| tired out | exhausto | n'en pouvoir plus | übermüdet | píjuàn |
| try on | probarse | essayer | anprobieren | shi-chuān |
| try out | probar | essayer | jemanden halten für | shi-yan |
| wear out | gastarse | user | abgetragen | shǐ moùrén jīnpí-lìjìn |

# 1–16 DOUBLE-DUTY WORDS: Words With Multiple Meanings

**arms**
He placed the child in her mother's *arms*.
The rebels needed to buy *arms* to fight the war.

**bail**
We had to *bail* to keep the boat from sinking.
She was released from jail when she paid $500 *bail*.

**ball**
The *ball* rolled under the table.
The women wore their prettiest dresses to the *ball*.

**bank**
You can cash your check at the *bank*.
We had a picnic on the *bank* of the river.

**bark**
Did you hear the dog *bark*?
The *bark* on the old tree is dry and brittle.

**bat**
A *bat* flew from the barn and frightened me.
The children played with the *bat* and ball.

**bit**
Jenn checked the *bit* in the horse's mouth.
I *bit* into the apple.
It will take just a *bit* longer.

**blow**
The wind began to *blow*, and the leaves fell.
The *blow* to his head knocked the fighter out.

**boil**
Alice showed the doctor the *boil* on her finger.
*Boil* some water for tea, please.

**bridge**
We crossed the *bridge* over the Raritan River.
*Bridge* is a card game for four people.

**case**
She put her eyeglasses in their *case*.
The lawyer won her first *case*.

**cleave**
We used the ax to *cleave* the wood.
The frightened children *cleaved* to the old woman.

**compound**
The soldiers surrounded the enemy *compound*.
A *compound* sentence is made of two clauses.

**count**
The duke, *count*, and earl received awards.
The child is learning to *count* from one to ten.

**cue**
The actor missed his *cue* and did not say his line.
He held the *cue* steady and aimed at the eight-ball.

**date**
Bill asked Sally for a *date*.
Today's *date* is March 28th.

**fair**
The weather was *fair* on the day of the race.
The judge's decision was *fair*.
We went on the rides at the *fair*.

**fan**
David is a baseball *fan*; he never misses a game.
It's very warm; please, turn on the *fan*.

| | |
|---|---|
| file | Put your papers in the *file*. |
| | The children marched in single *file*. |
| | The prisoner used a *file* to cut the metal bar. |
| firm | When he finished college, he joined a law *firm*. |
| | Apples should be *firm*, not soft. |
| fold | *Fold* your paper in half. |
| | The girl took care of the sheep in the *fold*. |
| game | It sounded exciting, so I was *game* to try it. |
| | Poker is his favorite card *game*. |
| hide | The belts were made from the *hide* of a cow. |
| | I usually *hide* the gifts for the children's birthdays. |
| grave | There was no laughter on the *grave* occasion. |
| | The coffin was lowered into the *grave*. |
| hold | The sailors put their supplies into the ship's *hold*. |
| | *Hold* the string or the balloon will drift away. |
| jam | I tried to *jam* one more coat into the full closet. |
| | We put strawberry *jam* on our toast. |
| | We were stuck in a traffic *jam* for an hour. |
| jar | The loud noise *jarred* the old man. |
| | Put the *jar* of mustard on the table. |
| kind | What *kind* of ice cream do you like? |
| | She was always *kind* and gentle. |
| last | I hope this will *last* until Tuesday. |
| | The *last* time I saw her she was very thin. |
| lean | He *leaned* against the building while he waited. |
| | The runner was tan and *lean* after the summer's races. |
| like | A briefcase is *like* a bookbag. |
| | I *like* fudge cookies. |
| line | We stood in *line* to get tickets. |
| | Write you name on the *line*. |
| long | I *long* to go to a quiet beach. |
| | How *long* is the story? |
| mean | What did you *mean* when you said that? |
| | He was *mean* and unkind. |
| | We calculated the *mean* score for the two teams. |
| mine | The silver ore is brought out of the *mine* in carts. |
| | Put your chair next to *mine*. |
| miss | *Miss* Sims is the new biology teacher. |
| | I will *miss* you when you move to the city. |
| net | The fish were caught in the *net*, not on hooks. |
| | After we paid the taxes, our *net* pay was $300. |

| | |
|---|---|
| palm | The gypsy looked at the lines on my *palm*.<br>We took many pictures of the *palm* trees in Florida. |
| pen | The pigs live in a *pen*.<br>Sign your name with this *pen*. |
| present | John was absent on Friday, not *present*.<br>For her birthday Jill received five *presents*. |
| press | The editor and other members of the *press* took notes.<br>Ask the tailor to *press* this skirt.<br>*Press* the button to start the machine. |
| punch | The *punch* was made from fruit juice and soda.<br>Josh *punched* the bag as hard as he could. |
| rare | I like my steak *rare*, not well done.<br>Only three people have ever owned this *rare* coin. |
| rest | Anna will do the *rest* of the shopping.<br>After the long walk up the hill, I wanted to *rest*. |
| seal | Don't use the medicine if the safety *seal* is broken.<br>We saw the *seals* at the zoo. |
| second | There are sixty *seconds* in a minute.<br>I was *second* today, but tomorrow I might be first. |
| sole | I ordered the *sole* for lunch because I like fish.<br>He was the *sole* survivor of the crash.<br>There was a hole in the *sole* of his shoe. |
| spell | The child learned to *spell* his name.<br>The witch put a magic *spell* on the tree. |
| stable | Put the horses in the *stable*.<br>He may leave the hospital if his breathing is *stable*. |
| steep | The mountain was *steep*, and the climb difficult.<br>We *steeped* the tea bag for three minutes. |
| stick | The glue was dried, and the stamp would not *stick*.<br>We collected *sticks* and leaves for the fire. |
| story | This is a five-*story* building.<br>Tell the children a bedtime *story*. |
| temple | He took two aspirin for the pain in his *temple*.<br>The men walked to the *temple* to pray. |
| tick | *Ticks* are insects that spread Lyme's Disease.<br>Can you hear the clock *tick*? |
| tire | I never *tire* of hearing my favorite music.<br>I had a flat *tire* on my new car. |
| vault | The athlete *vaulted* the six-foot barrier with ease.<br>The actress put her diamond jewelry in the *vault*. |
| wake | Be quiet or you will *wake* the baby.<br>The waves in the *wake* of the speedboat were very high. |

*The ESL Teacher's Book of Lists,* © 1993 by John Wiley & Sons, Inc.

well        I feel very *well* today.
                  The boy put the bucket into the *well* to get water.

will         The lawyer wrote a *will* for the old man before he died.
                  I *will* see the man tomorrow, not today.

yard        A *yard* is equal to thirty-six inches.
                  We had a picnic in the *yard.*

ability, power, skill, talent, aptitude

able, adept, adroit, skillful, talented

about, almost, nearly, near, approximately

accident, disaster, mishap, incident, calamity

achievement, feat, accomplishment, attainment, fulfillment

agree, consent, assent, concede, concur

anger, ire, displeasure, animosity, rage

answer, respond, reply, retort, rejoin

ask, beg, request, implore, beseech

bizarre, odd, weird, exotic, peculiar

bother, annoy, vex, irritate, disturb

brave, bold, daring, adventurous, courageous

cheap, low-cost, inexpensive, economical, reasonable

correct, true, accurate, exact, faultless

crazy, mad, insane, lunatic, demented

do, act, perform, execute, accomplish

empty, vacant, void, unoccupied, unfilled

enemy, adversary, foe, rival, antagonist

excitement, gusto, zest, flavor, pleasure

fair, just, fitting, proper, equitable

fat, obese, fleshy, corpulent, plump

fight, disagree, brawl, feud, quarrel

fix, mend, repair, amend, restore

friend, pal, companion, classmate, acquaintance

game, sport, recreation, pastime, amusement

good, virtuous, honorable, pious, upright

happy, cheerful, merry, joyous, ecstatic

hard, difficult, perplexing, arduous, troublesome

hate, detest, abhor, despise, loathe

help, aid, assist, foster, support

hit, beat, strike, pound, thrash

holy, religious, pious, saintly, devout

honest, open, candid, frank, truthful

hurt, injure, abuse, mistreat, damage

idea, notion, concept, principle, thought

important, significant, relevant, leading, essential

*The ESL Teacher's Book of Lists,* © 1993 by John Wiley & Sons, Inc.

invent, design, devise, construct, create

job, employment, occupation, profession, work

large, great, huge, immense, gigantic

law, rule, edict, regulation, principle

love, affection, attachment, passion, devotion

near, adjoining, neighboring, adjacent, bordering

price, cost, value, worth, expense

quick, fleet, nimble, agile, swift

quiet, still, hushed, silent, tranquil

religion, faith, belief, creed, doctrine

report, announce, proclaim, declare, notify

same, uniform, unvarying, homogeneous, equivalent

see, view, perceive, apprehend, notice

shape, form, mold, design, fashion

show, present, display, exhibit, demonstrate

sly, sneaky, cunning, crafty, artful

spirit, life, vitality, energy, enthusiasm

stay, remain, wait, rest, dwell

story, account, report, narration, description

strange, abnormal, unusual, irregular, atypical

strict, stern, severe, rigid, harsh

strong, powerful, robust, hearty, brawny

stupid, dull, incompetent, senseless, obtuse

sure, certain, assured, confident, positive

surprise, amazement, awe, astonishment, bewilderment

swift, speedy, fast, lively, rapid

take, grab, seize, grasp, snatch

teach, educate, instruct, train, develop

travel, trip, expedition, voyage, journey

try, attempt, endeavor, strive, undertake

wide, vast, spacious, boundless, prodigious

wise, sage, sensible, intelligent, learned

# 1–18 OPPOSITES ATTRACT:
## *Antonyms*

| | | | |
|---|---|---|---|
| above | below | high | low |
| add | subtract | in | out |
| all | none | left | right |
| always | never | light | dark |
| arrive | leave | long | short |
| back | front | lost | found |
| before | after | loud | soft |
| begin | end | love | hate |
| big | little | many | few |
| black | white | more | less |
| boy | girl | morning | evening |
| come | go | most | least |
| dark | light | near | far |
| day | night | new | old |
| dead | alive | old | new |
| deep | shallow | on | off |
| empty | full | open | close |
| even | odd | over | under |
| fast | slow | right | wrong |
| fat | thin | same | different |
| find | lose | sharp | dull |
| first | last | small | large |
| floor | ceiling | something | nothing |
| friend | enemy | start | stop |
| give | get | tall | short |
| go | stop | then | now |
| good | bed | to | from |
| happy | sad | together | apart |
| hard | soft | top | bottom |
| he | she | up | down |
| heaven | hell | wet | dry |
| heavy | light | with | without |
| here | there | yes | no |

*The ESL Teacher's Book of Lists,* © 1993 by John Wiley & Sons, Inc.

# 1-19 TWO FOR ONE:
## English/Spanish Cognates

| English | Spanish | English | Spanish |
|---------|---------|---------|---------|
| abdomen | abdomen | anatomy | anatomía |
| abhor | aborrercer | animal | animal |
| abort | abortar | annual | anual |
| absolute | absoluto | April | abril |
| absorb | absorber | arid | árido |
| absorbent | absorbente | arrogant | arrogante |
| abstract | abstracto | assembly | asamblea |
| absurd | absurdo | attraction | atracción |
| acceleration | aceleración | austere | austero |
| accent | acento | authority | autoridad |
| accessory | accesorio | balance | balanza |
| accident | accidente | bank | banco |
| accidental | accidental | bar | barra |
| accompany | acompañar | billion | billón |
| acid | ácido | biography | biografía |
| acre | acre | biology | biología |
| active | activo | block | bloque |
| actor | actor | brutal | brutal |
| actress | actriz | calcium | calcio |
| adhere | adherirse | calendar | calendario |
| adhesion | adhesión | calm | calma |
| administer | administrar | cancel | cancelar |
| adminstration | administración | candle | candela |
| admiration | admiración | canoe | canoa |
| admire | admirar | capital | capital |
| admission | admisión | captain | capitán |
| adolescent | adolescente | carpenter | carpintero |
| adore | adorar | category | categoría |
| adult | adulto | | |
| adverb | adverbio | | |
| adversary | adversario | | |
| adverse | adverso | | |
| affirm | afirmar | | |
| affirmative | afirmativo | | |
| agility | agilidad | | |
| agony | agonía | | |
| agriculture | agricultura | | |
| allergy | alergia | | |
| alphabet | alfabeto | | |
| alter | alterar | | |
| ambiguous | ambiguo | | |
| ambition | ambición | | |
| ample | amplio | | |

| English | Spanish | English | Spanish |
|---|---|---|---|
| central | central | human | humano |
| character | carácter | hysterical | histérico |
| characteristic | característico | idea | idea |
| chocolate | chocolate | idol | ídolo |
| circulation | circulación | illegal | ilegal |
| circumstance | circunstancia | illusion | ilusión |
| clinic | clínica | imagine | imaginar |
| colony | colonia | impressive | impresionante |
| comic | cómico | inclination | inclinación |
| commercial | comercial | index | índice |
| concise | conciso | individual | individuo |
| confidence | confidencia | insect | insecto |
| conflict | conflicto | intense | intenso |
| constant | constante | invent | inventar |
| construction | construcción | involve | envolver |
| credit | crédito | journal | jornal |
| crystal | cristal | kerosene | kerosina |
| culture | cultura | labor | labor |
| defend | defender | laboratory | laboratorio |
| democracy | democracia | legal | legal |
| department | departmento | license | licencia |
| destruction | destrucción | literature | literatura |
| determine | determinar | magnetic | magnético |
| direction | dirección | magnificent | magnífico |
| director | director | mania | manía |
| dormitory | dormitorio | manual | manual |
| economy | economia | manuscript | manuscrito |
| education | educación | mark | marca |
| energy | energía | mathematics | matemáticas |
| excellence | excelencia | matrix | matriz |
| exhibition | exhibición | melon | melón |
| extreme | extremo | mercury | mercurio |
| factor | factor | mineral | mineral |
| fault | falta | minute | minuto |
| fragile | frágil | model | modelo |
| fragment | fragmento | molecule | molécula |
| friction | fricción | moral | moral |
| function | función | morbid | mórbido |
| gallon | galón | motor | motor |
| gas | gas | music | música |
| general | general | national | nacional |
| gradual | gradual | natural | natural |
| habit | hábito | notice | noticia |
| history | historia | number | número |
| honor | honrar | object | objetar |
| horror | horror | observe | observar |
| hospital | hospital | offensive | ofensivo |

*The ESL Teacher's Book of Lists,* © 1993 by John Wiley & Sons, Inc.

| English | Spanish | English | Spanish |
|---|---|---|---|
| official | oficial | recommend | recomendar |
| opinion | opinión | refine | refinar |
| optimism | optimismo | reform | reforma |
| oral | oral | remedy | remedio |
| oval | oval | represent | representar |
| oxygen | oxígeno | republic | república |
| pajamas | pijama | reside | residir |
| palace | palacio | respond | responder |
| parade | parada | result | resulta |
| part | parte | revoke | revocar |
| partial | parcial | revolutionary | revolucionario |
| participate | participar | robust | robusto |
| pass | pasar | romantic | romántico |
| passion | pasión | salmon | salmón |
| pasture | pastura | sandal | sandalia |
| pause | pausa | satellite | satélite |
| perfume | perfume | secretary | secretario |
| permit | permitir | segment | segmento |
| person | persona | series | serie |
| petition | petición | simple | simple |
| pharmacy | farmacia | siren | sirena |
| planet | planeta | solar | solar |
| plate | plato | solid | sólido |
| platform | plataforma | solo | solo |
| pleasant | placentero | special | especial |
| poet | poeta | suburb | suburbio |
| politics | política | supreme | supremo |
| practice | práctica | taxi | taxi |
| prefer | preferir | telephone | teléfono |
| preliminary | preliminar | television | televisión |
| premise | premisa | tennis | tenis |
| president | presidente | terrific | terrífico |
| prevention | prevención | tobacco | tabaco |
| principal | principal | traitor | traidor |
| process | proceso | tranquil | tranquilo |
| producer | productor | tunnel | túnel |
| product | producto | uniform | uniforme |
| pronounce | pronunciar | union | unión |
| proportion | proporción | urban | urbano |
| protest | protestar | vacant | vacante |
| provision | provisión | vacation | vacación |
| prudent | prudente | verbal | verbal |
| public | público | vision | visión |
| punctual | puntual | visit | visita |
| radio | radio | volume | volumen |
| rational | racional | yard | yarda |
| reason | razón | zone | zona |

# 1–20 *TWO FOR ONE:*
## *English/French Cognates*

| English | French | English | French |
|---|---|---|---|
| **English** | **French** | **English** | **French** |
| absolutely | absolument | elementary | élémentaire |
| accent | un accent | error | une erreur |
| accept | accepter | excellent | excellent |
| activity | l'activité | except | excepter |
| admire | admirer | exercise | un exercice |
| adult | une adulte | fatigued | fatigué |
| agency | l'agence | finish | finir |
| agreeable | agréable | flatterer | le flatteur |
| aid | aider | fruit | les fruits |
| animal | l'animal | government | le gouvernement |
| apartment | un appartement | hello | allô |
| applaud | applaudir | hospital | hôpital |
| arrive | arriver | hotel | hôtel |
| arrange | arranger | illuminated | illuminé |
| artist | l'artiste | impatient | impatient |
| aspirin | l'aspirine | insist | insister |
| autumn | l'automne | invite | inviter |
| avenue | une avenue | jacket | la jaquette |
| banana | une banane | lamp | la lampe |
| bank | la banque | lesson | la leçon |
| beauty | la beauté | letter | la lettre |
| bicycle | la bicyclette | liberty | la liberté |
| blouse | la blouse | machine | la machine |
| blue | bleu | magnificent | magnifique |
| calendar | le calendrier | marriage | le mariage |
| center | le centre | May | mai |
| change | changement | menu | le menu |
| check | le cheque | message | le message |
| chocolate | le chocolat | million | le million |
| color | la couleur | modern | moderne |
| comfortable | comfortable | monument | le monument |
| composition | la composition | music | musique |
| continue | continuer | naturally | naturellement |
| cousin | le cousin | no | non |
| dance | danser | November | novembre |
| December | décembre | obey | obéir |
| decision | la décision | omelet | une omelette |
| dentist | le dentiste | orange | une orange |
| dessert | le dessert | page | la page |
| detail | le détail | parents | mes parents |
| dictionary | le dictionnaire | park | le parc |
| dinner | le dîner | passport | le passeport |
| elegant | élégant | pay | payer |

| English | French | English | Frenc |
|---|---|---|---|
| perfume | le parfum | telephone | le téléphone |
| pharmacy | la pharmacie | toast | des toasts |
| photograph | la photographie | tomato | la tomate |
| poet | le poète | train | le train |
| prepare | préparer | uncle | l'oncle |
| pretend | prétendre | university | la université |
| professor | le professeur | vacation | les vacances |
| program | le programme | zero | zéro |
| radio | la radio | | |
| reserve | réserver | | |
| respond | répondre | | |
| restaurant | le restaurant | | |
| ridiculous | ridicule | | |
| salad | une salade | | |
| sandwich | le sandwich | | |
| scene | la scène | | |
| science | la science | | |
| September | septembre | | |
| sign | signer | | |
| society | la société | | |
| soup | la soupe | | |
| statue | la statue | | |
| surely | sûrement | | |
| sweater | le sweater | | |
| table | la table | | |
| tea | thé | | |

*le téléphone*

# 1-21 TWO FOR ONE:
## English/German Cognates

| English | German | English | German |
|---------|--------|---------|--------|
| address | Adresse | blond | blond |
| alcohol | Alkohol | bus | Bus |
| all | alle | cafe | Cafe |
| analysis | Analyse | canal | Kanal |
| anatomy | Anatomie | centimeter | Zentimeter |
| April | April | chance | Chance |
| archaeology | Archäologie | cigarette | Zigarette |
| argument | Argument | club | Club |
| arm | Arm | computer | Computer |
| athlete | Athlet | conservative | konservativ |
| August | August | control | kontrollieren |
| auto | Auto | cost | kosten |
| bakery | Bäckerie | December | Dezember |
| band | Band | director | Direktor |
| bank | Bank | discipline | Disziplin |
| bar | Barre | dumb | dumm |
| barrier | Barriere | elegant | elegant |
| beer | Bier | Europe | Europa |
| begin | beginnen | family | Familie |
| best | besten | fan | Fan |
| biology | Biologie | finger | Finger |
| | | frost | Frost |
| | | garden | Garten |
| | | gold | Gold |
| | | hand | Hand |
| | | hello | hallo |
| | | here | hier |
| | | hobby | Hobby |
| | | hotel | Hotel |
| | | humor | Humor |
| | | idea | Idee |
| | | idol | Idol |
| | | illustrate | illustrieren |
| | | industry | Industrie |
| | | instrument | Instrument |
| | | intelligent | intelligent |
| | | international | international |
| | | jeans | Jeans |
| | | journalist | Journalist |
| | | legal | legal |
| | | lemonade | Limonade |
| | | make | machen |

| English | German | English | German |
|---|---|---|---|
| meter | Meter | rock concert | Rockkonzert |
| million | Million | rock group | Rockgruppe |
| minimum | Minimum | sandal | Sandale |
| minute | Minute | send | senden |
| moment | Moment | September | September |
| moral | Moral | siren | Sirene |
| name | Name | situation | Situation- |
| nation | Nation | comedy | komödie |
| nature | Natur | social | sozial |
| new | neu | sport | Sport |
| November | November | state | Staat |
| October | Oktober | taxi | Taxi |
| often | oft | tea | Tee |
| orchestra | Orchester | telephone | Telefon |
| park | Park | theater | Theater |
| partner | Partner | theory | Theorie |
| passive | passiv | tourist | Tourist |
| pause | Pause | unconventional | unkonven- |
| person | Person | | tionell |
| phonograph | Phonograph | university | Universität |
| plan | Plan | volleyball | Volleyball |
| popular | popular | waltz | Walzer |
| press | Presse | west | Westen |
| professor | Professor | winter | Winter |
| program | Programm | work | Werk |
| quiz | Quiz | zenith | Zenit |

# SECTION 2
# Academic Vocabulary

# 2–1 OFF TO SCHOOL:
## Classroom and School Vocabulary

absent
achievement test
administration
advanced placement
advisor
aide
assembly
assignment
attendance
auditorium
backpack
ballpoint
bathroom
bell
blackboard
book
book room
bookstore
boys' room
bus pass
cafeteria
campus
cassette tape
class discussion
classroom
club
co-ed
coach
combination lock
computer lab
dance
dean
desk
detention
dictionary
dismissal
education
enroll
ESL program
exam
examples
exercises
extracurricular
  activity

faculty
fail
finals
fire drill
flunk
game
girls' room
grades
graduate
graduation
guidance counselor
guidance office
gym
gymnasium
half-day
hall pass
headphone
headset
highlighter
holiday
homeroom
homework
honor roll
honors class
instructor
janitor
lab
laboratory
language lab
language proficiency
  test
lavatory
learn
lecture

librarian
library
locker
locker room
looseleaf paper
lunch
map
marker
marking period
media center
midterms
note
notebook
nurse
nurse's office
open house
orientation
P.T.A.
pad
party
pass
pen
pencil
pencil sharpener
period
permission slip
placement test
playground
present

principal
probation
professor
prom
pupil
quiz
recess
remedial
report card
resource room
ruler
schedule
school

school bus
school secretary
scores
seat
security guard
snow day
stage
student
study hall
superintendent
tardy
teach
teacher

teachers' room
team
term
test
textbook
theater
truant
tutor
vacation
vice-principal
warning notice
workbook

**Course Titles**

algebra
American govern-
  ment
art
basic math
bilingual
biology
Black studies
bookkeeping
business English
business math
calculus
chemistry
civics
composition
computer science
cooperative
  education
dance
data processing
drama
driver's education

Earth science
English
ESL - English as a
  Second Language
European history
foreign language
French
general math
geography
geometry
German
gym
health
history
home economics
industrial education
Italian
Latin
literature
mathematics
music
philosophy

phys. ed.
physical education
physical science
physics
precalculus
psychology
science
shop
social studies
sociology
Spanish
spelling
steno
technical education
trigonometry
typing
U.S. history
vocational
  education
world history

**Types of Schools**

private school
public school
day-care center
nursery school
kindergarten
preschool
elementary school

middle school
intermediate school
junior high school
secondary school
senior high school
regional high school
vocational school

technical school
trade school
junior college
community college
college
university

*The ESL Teacher's Book of Lists*, © 1993 by John Wiley & Sons, Inc.

**Common Idioms**

to be absent

to be present

to be tardy

to call the roll

to collect homework

to collect the papers

to copy

to cram

to cut class

to daydream

to demonstrate

to dictate

to discuss

to do an assignment

to do an example

to do homework

to do math

to do research

to erase the board

to learn

to lecture

to line up

to listen carefully

to memorize

to pass

to pass the papers
 out

to pay attention

to play a tape

to play hookey

to print

to read

to report to the office

to salute the flag

to sign

to sign in

to sign up

to study

to take a course

to take a test

to take an exam

to take attendance

to take notes

to take ——— (a
 course)

to talk about

to type

to write

to write on the
 board

## 2–2  ONE PLUS ONE:
### Basic Mathematics Vocabulary

add
addition
alike
all
amount
angle
area
average
between
both
center
centimeter
change
circle
circumference
column
combine
common factor
common multiple
compare
cone
congruent
connect
contain
cost
count
counting numbers
cube
curve
cylinder
decimal
degree
denominator
diagonal
diameter
difference
digit
distance
divide
division
divisor
double
each

element
equal
equals
equation
equivalent
estimate
even number
factor
fewer
figure
first
foot
fraction
gallon
geometry
gram

graph
greater than
group
half
height
horizontal
hour
identify
inch
inequality
inside
intersect
kilogram
kilometer
least
length

less
less than
line
liter
many
match
measure
median
metric
middle
mile
minus
minute
missing
mixed
more
most
multiple
multiplication
multiply
name
negative
number
number line
numerator
odd
odd number
one-to-one
operation
opposite
order
ounce
parallel
parenthesis
percent
perimeter
perpendicular
place value
plane
plus
point
positive
prime number

The ESL Teacher's Book of Lists, © 1993 by John Wiley & Sons, Inc.

| | | |
|---|---|---|
| problem | same | sum |
| product | second | table |
| property | sequence | times |
| protractor | side | total |
| quart | sign | triangle |
| radius | similar | unequal |
| range | simple | unit |
| ratio | single | unknown |
| ray | solution | value |
| reciprocal | solve | vertical |
| rectangle | some | volume |
| remainder | sphere | whole number |
| rename | square | yard |
| right angle | straight | zero |
| round | subtract | |
| row | subtraction | |

# 2-3 ADDING IT UP:
## Intermediate/Advanced Mathematics Vocabulary

abscissa
absolute
adjacent
alternate
altitude
angle
approximately
arc
axis
bisect
calculate
capacity
complementary
computation
consecutive
constant
construct
corresponding
decimal
decrease
denominator
determine
diameter
equality
equilateral

estimate
exponent
express
exterior
factor
finite
graph
greater than
improper
increase
infinite
integer
interest
interior
intersect
inverse
isosceles
least
less than
line
lowest
maximum
mean
minimum
multiple

negative
numeral
numerator
obtuse
odd
perfect
pi
plot
prime
quadrant
radius
right
scientific
segment
simplest
simplify
square
squared
supplementary
tangent
theorem
triangle
union
variable
vertical

# 2–4 HOW DOES IT WORK?: Basic Science Vocabulary

absorb
accurate
adaptation
air
air current
air pressure
algae
amoeba
amphibian
ancestor
apply
atmosphere
atom
bacteria
balance
barometer
battery
boil
carbon dioxide
cell
Celsius
chemical
chlorine
chlorophyll
circuit
circulation

classify
cloud
community
compass
compound
condense
control
core
crust
current
degree
density
desert
dew
digestion
disease
dissolve
distance
earth
eclipse
electricity
element
energy
environment
erosion
evaporate
evidence
expand
extinct
Fahrenheit
food chain
force
friction
frost
fuel
gas
gravity
habitat
heat
image
instinct
length
lens

liquid
magnet
mantle
mass
matter
melting point
microscope
mineral
moisture
molecule
moon
motion
nucleus
orbit
organism
oxygen
physical
planet
pollute
power
predict
property
protein
prove
range
rate
reaction
respiration
revolve
rock
season
sediment
sense
solid
solution
sound
space
system
temperature
thermometer
thunder
tides
weight

# 2–5   WHAT'S A LITTLE MUTATION?:
## Intermediate/Advanced Science Vocabulary

absolute zero
absorb
accelerate
accuracy
acid
adhesion
adsorption
aequeous solutions
alcohol
alkali
alloy
alpha particles
alternating
aluminum
amino acid
ammonia
ampere
amplitude
analysis
anatomy
aorta
artery
ascorbic acid
asexual
assimilation
atomic
autonomic
barometer
base
beta particles

biome
bonding
Boyle's Law
calcium
calorie
carbon
catalysts
cell
centripetal force
charge
chemical change
chlorine
chromosome
cilia
coefficients
cohesion
combustion
condensation
conductor
convection
convergence
crystal
cycle
cytology
decomposition
dehydration
dendrite
dispersion
dissect
distance

distillation
divergence
dominant
dry ice
ecology
ecosystem
electrodes
electrolyte
electromagnetic
electron
element
embryo
endocrine
entropy
enzyme
equilibrium
eugenics
euthenics
evolution
fiber optics
fision
fluid
fluorescence
formula
frequency
fusion
gamete
gene
genetics
germination

The ESL Teacher's Book of Lists, © 1993 by John Wiley & Sons, Inc.

gestation
glucose
habitat
half-life
heredity
heterozygous
hormone
host
hydrocarbon
hydrochloric acid
hydrogen
hypothesis
inertia
inorganic
inverse
ions
joule
kinetic
laser
litmus
magnetic
metabolism
mitosis
molecules
monozygous
mutation
nerves
neuron
nitrogen

ohm
parallax
organic
osmosis
ovum
oxidation
oxides
oxygen
periodic table
petri dish
pH
photosynthesis
phylogeny
phylum
physical change
potassium
pressure
protein
quark
reaction
recessive
resistance
saturation
scientific notation
sodium
solar
soluble
species
spectroscope

spectrum
speed
sperm
sulfur
superconductivity
symbiosis
symmetry
synapse
taxonomy
test tube
tissue
titration
transfer
transmutation
unsaturated
vacuum
valence
vapor
velocity
vibration
vitamin
volt
volume
wavelength
work
yeast
zygote

# 2–6 WHAT IN THE WORLD?: Basic Social Studies Vocabulary

abolish
Abraham Lincoln
administration
Africa
ally
amendment
ancestor
ancient
area
artifact
Asia
assembly
Atlantic Ocean
authority
balance
beliefs
Benjamin Franklin
bill
Bill of Rights
branch
British
cabinet
candidate
capital
capitalism
charter
Christopher
  Columbus
city
civil
Civil War
civilization
colonists
colony
communist
community
compromise
confederate
Congress
Constitution
continent
country
culture

customs
declaration
democracy
democrat
direction
distance
election
Europe
executive
expedition
explorer
federal
freedom
French
frontier
geography
George Washington
government
governor
harbor
history
homestead
immigrant
indentured servant
independence

Industrial Revolution
invention
judicial
justice
law
legal
legislative
Lief Erikson
majority
map
Mexico
minority
monarch
monarchy
mountain
national
native
North America
ocean
Pacific Ocean
Parliament
patriot
pilgrim
pioneer
policy
political
possession
prejudice
president
primary
prohibit
puritan
represent
republic
republican
river
sea
senate
slavery
society
South America
Spanish
state

| | | |
|---|---|---|
| system | treaty | voyage |
| taxation | union | Washington, D.C. |
| Thomas Jefferson | unite | wilderness |
| time line | veto | worship |
| trade | vote | Yankee |

# 2-7 OF THE PEOPLE:
## Intermediate/Advanced Social Studies Vocabulary

alien
alliance
annex
apartheid
armistice
capitalism
civil rights
cold war
colonialism
communism
convention
crisis
delegates
depression
dictator
document
economy
electoral
emancipation
emigration

expedition
fascism
federalism
filibuster
foreign
granges
impeach
inaugurate
invasion
Iron Curtain
isolationism
judiciary
labor unions
laissez faire
liberal
migrants
Monroe Doctrine
NATO
Nazism
petition

pocket veto
poll tax
preamble
primary
recession
reconstruction
referendum
reservations
revolution
riots
secede
segregate
separation
socialism
strike
tariff
treason
unanimous
United Nations

The ESL Teacher's Book of Lists, © 1993 by John Wiley & Sons, Inc.

# SECTION 3
# Grammar

# 3–1  BUILDING BLOCKS:
## *The Parts of Speech*

The English language has eight major word groups, or parts of speech:

| | | | |
|---|---|---|---|
| noun | adjective | verb | preposition |
| pronoun | conjunction | adverb | interjection |

They are the building blocks of the language and are used in certain set patterns. These patterns form the grammar or syntax of both written and spoken English.

## NOUN

A **noun** names or points out a person, place, thing, or idea. It can act or be acted upon. Examples: *teacher, home, bike, democracy.*

A **proper noun** names a specific person, place, or thing. Always capitalize a proper noun. Examples: *Jennifer, New Jersey, North Sea, Eiffel Tower, Central Park.*

A **common noun** names one of a class or group of persons, places, or things. Common nouns are not capitalized. Examples: *boy, president, state, sea, building.*

In sentences nouns are used as subjects, direct objects, indirect objects, or objects of prepositions:

| | |
|---|---|
| Subject | The *dog* barked. |
| Direct Object | John broke the *lock*. |
| Indirect Object | I gave *Christine* the book. |
| Object of Preposition | We went to the *park*. |

## PRONOUN

A pronoun is used in place of a noun. Different pronoun forms are used to show person (first, second, or third person), number (singular or plural), gender (masculine, feminine, or neuter), and case (nominative, possessive, or objective).

There are personal, interrogative, relative, indefinite, demonstrative, and reflexive pronouns. Examples: *it, we, who, which, anyone, that, ourselves.*

(See "The Pro's" and "Yours and Mine.")

## ADJECTIVE

An adjective is a word that is used to describe a noun or a pronoun, and tells what kind, how many, or which one.

EXAMPLES: *lazy, beautiful, three, that.*

(See "Which One Has More?")

## VERB

A verb is a word that shows a physical or mental action, or the state of being of a subject.

EXAMPLES:  *sit, think, swim, breathe, appear, know.*

A **transitive** verb relates an action that has an object. Example: Ellen *baked the bread.* An **intransitive** verb does not have an object. Example: The baby *cried.* A **linking** verb connects the subject and complement that describes or relates back to the subject. Example: The old *man seems tired.*

A **regular** verb forms its past form and past participle by adding the suffix -d or -ed to the verb base. Examples: *look, looked, looked; thank, thanked, thanked.* An **irregular** verb does not. Their past forms and past participles do not follow a pattern and must be learned. Examples: *go, went, gone; see, saw, seen; bite, bit, bitten.*

An **auxiliary** verb, also called a helping verb, is used with the main verb to show tense and mood. Examples: *will* go, *has been* crying, *had gone.* A **modal auxiliary** verb is used to indicate possibility, need, ability, willingness, or obligation. Modals include *can, could, should, may, might, must, ought, shall, will, would.*

EXAMPLES:  You *may* stay out late. I *ought* to call home. He *must* leave now.

A verb is in the **active** voice when the subject is the doer or agent of the action. Example: Marie *baked* the pie. A verb is in the **passive** voice when the subject is the receiver of the action. Example: The pie *was baked* by Marie.
(See "Yesterday, Today, and Tomorrow.")

## ADVERB

An adverb describes a verb, an adjective, or another adverb by providing information about where, when, how, how much, or to what extent. Many adverbs are formed by adding the suffix -ly to an adjective or noun.

EXAMPLES:  *outside, later, seriously, few.*

(See "Where, When, and How.")

## CONJUNCTION

A word that is used to join words, phrases, or clauses.

EXAMPLES:  *and, because, however, but.*

(See "And or But?")

*The ESL Teacher's Book of Lists,* © 1993 by John Wiley & Sons, Inc.

## PREPOSITION

A word that is used to show the relationship of a noun or pronoun to another word. A prepositional phrase is made up of a preposition, a noun and noun modifiers, if any. In a sentence, prepositional phrases may indicate an indirect object or act as adverbs of time or place.

> EXAMPLES: *to* the girl (indirect object), *on* the bed (adverb), *across* the street (adverb), *before* noon (adverb).

These are the most commonly used prepositions:

| | | | |
|---|---|---|---|
| about | behind | from | throughout |
| above | below | in | to |
| across | beneath | into | toward |
| after | beside | near | under |
| against | between | of | underneath |
| along | beyond | off | until |
| amid | by | on | up |
| among | down | over | upon |
| around | during | past | with |
| at | except | since | within |
| before | for | through | without |

(See "Where, When, and How.")

## INTERJECTION

A word that is used alone to express strong emotion.

> EXAMPLES: *Oh! Congratulations! Damn! Bravo!*

# 3–2 WHERE, WHEN, AND HOW: *Adverbs and Adverbial Phrases*

Adverbs describe verbs, adjectives, or other adverbs by providing information about where, when, how, or how much. Adverbs can be single words, phrases, or clauses.

Many adverbs are formed by adding the suffix *-ly* to adjectives, but not all words (e.g. friendly, lively, deadly, and princely).

| adjective | + | -ly | = | adverb |
|-----------|---|-----|---|--------|
| correct | | -ly | | *correctly* |
| dainty | | -ly | | *daintily* |
| stern | | -ly | | *sternly* |
| serious | | -ly | | *seriously* |
| speedy | | -ly | | *speedily* |

An adverb can show the degree to which a quality is associated with the verb, an adjective, or another adverb it is modifying by using one of three forms: positive, comparative, and superlative.

The **comparative** form adds *-er* to the adverb or adds the word "more" before the adverb. The comparative form is used to compare the verb modified to one other verb. Examples:

| soon | *sooner* | powerfully | *more powerfully* |
|------|----------|------------|-------------------|

The **superlative** form adds *-est* to the adverb or adds the word "most" before the adverb. The superlative form is used to compare the verb modified to two or more other verbs. Examples:

| late | *latest* | stubbornly | *most stubbornly* |
|------|----------|------------|-------------------|

Most one-syllable and some two-syllable adverbs use *-er* and *-est* and longer adverbs use "*more*" and "*most*."

| Positive | I expect Kelly to arrive *soon*. |
| Comparative | I expect Kelly to arrive *sooner* than Elise. |
| Superlative | I expect Kelly to arrive the *soonest* of the three. |

| Positive | Roger spoke *sternly* to the driver. |
| Comparative | Roger spoke *more sternly* than Hal. |
| Superlative | Roger spoke *most sternly* of all the riders. |

Adverbs can also show negative comparisons. To form the negative comparative form use "less" with the adverb; to form the negative superlative form use "least" with the adverb. Examples:

| often | *less often* | *least often* |
|-------|--------------|---------------|
| clearly | *less clearly* | *least clearly* |
| quickly | *less quickly* | *least quickly* |

Not all adverbs follow these rules. Some have irregular comparisons, such as:

| *well* | *better* | *best* |
|--------|----------|--------|
| *badly* | *worse* | *worst* |

*The ESL Teacher's Book of Lists,* © 1993 by John Wiley & Sons, Inc.

and some have only one form. For example:

| | | |
|---|---|---|
| *afterward* | *inside* | *outside* |
| *nearby* | *away* | *here* |
| *there* | *downstairs* | *uptown* |
| *never* | *seldom* | *sometimes* |
| *infinitely* | *habitually* | *always* |
| *constantly* | *perpetually* | *everywhere* |

Adverbial phrases (also known as prepositional phrases) or clauses frequently begin with these prepositions:

| | |
|---|---|
| above | He put the sign *above* the doorbell. |
| across | The plane flew *across* the desert. |
| after | *After* we finished the game, we drove to the beach. |
| along | We ran *along* the shore each morning. |
| at | I asked him to meet me *at* the gym. |
| before | Jenn has to leave *before* we do. |
| behind | David put his backpack *behind* the desk. |
| beneath | The steward put my suitcase *beneath* the seat. |
| beside | I parked my car *beside* the trailer. |
| between | John is standing *between* Mary and Phil. |
| during | Not a sound was heard *during* her speech. |
| in | The lion paced *in* the cage. |
| in front | He asked the shortest person to stand *in front.* |
| near | The dog slept peacefully *near* the boy's bed. |
| on | He placed his trophy *on* the shelf. |
| over | We tossed the rope *over* the fence. |
| since | The house has been empty *since* Robert left. |
| to | The bubbles rose *to* the top of the liquid. |
| with | He announced the winners *with* pleasure. |
| within | The card was tucked *within* the folds of paper. |

*The ESL Teacher's Book of Lists,* © 1993 by John Wiley & Sons, Inc.

# 3–3  WHICH ONE HAS MORE?: *Adjectives*

An adjective is a word that is used to describe a noun or pronoun and tells what kind, how many, or points out which one. Adjectives can be single words, phrases, or clauses. Adjective phrases are also called adjectival phrases. Examples:

| what kind | how many | which one |
|---|---|---|
| lazy | several | this |
| of great value | three | that was painted red |
| powerful | few | those |

A **descriptive** adjective tells about a quality of the noun. Examples: *pretty* girl, *soft* pillow, *yellow* ribbon.

A **limiting** adjective narrows the noun or concept being told about; possessive adjectives, demonstrative adjectives and interrogative adjectives limit nouns. Examples: *his* sweater, *several* chairs, *whose* sandwich.

A **proper** adjective is derived from a proper noun. Examples: *Italian* bread, *Irish* coffee.

An adjective can show the degree to which a quality is associated with the noun or pronoun it is modifying by using one of three forms: positive, comparative, or superlative.

The **comparative** form adds -*er* to the adjective or adds the word *more* before the adjective. The comparative form is used to compare the noun or pronoun modified to one other noun or pronoun. Examples:

> pretty    *prettier*    powerful    *more powerful*

The **superlative** form adds -*est* to the adjective or adds the word *most* before the adjective. The superlative form is used to compare the noun or pronoun modified to two or more other nouns or pronouns. Examples:

> tall    *tallest*    stubborn    *most stubborn*

Most one-syllable and some two-syllable adjectives use -*er* and -*est* and longer adjectives use *more* and *most*.

| | |
|---|---|
| Positive | Dennis is a *lazy* boy. |
| Comparative | Dennis is *lazier* than Elise. |
| Superlative | Dennis is the *laziest* of the three children. |

| | |
|---|---|
| Positive | The *famous* skater won the gold medal. |
| Comparative | The *more famous* skater of the two won. |
| Superlative | The *most famous* skater of the three won. |

Adjectives can also show a **negative comparison**. To form the negative comparative form use "less" with the adjective; to form the negative superlative form use "least" with the adjective. Examples:

*The ESL Teacher's Book of Lists*, © 1993 by John Wiley & Sons, Inc.

| | | |
|---|---|---|
| eager | *less eager* | *least eager* |
| tired | *less tired* | *least tired* |
| drastic | *less drastic* | *least drastic* |

Not all adjectives follow these rules. Some have irregular comparisons, such as:

| | | |
|---|---|---|
| *good* | *better* | *best* |
| *bad* | *worse* | *worst* |

and some have only one form. For example:

| | | |
|---|---|---|
| *dead* | *pregnant* | *perfect* |
| *infinite* | *perpetual* | *alive* |

# 3–4 THE PRO'S:
## Pronouns

A pronoun is used in place of a noun. Different forms are used to show person, number, gender, and case. There are personal, interrogative, relative, indefinite, demonstrative, and reflexive pronouns.

A **personal** pronoun refers to one or more individuals or things. Personal pronouns may be in the nominative, objective, or possessive case.

| Singular | Nominative | Objective | Possessive |
|---|---|---|---|
| 1st person | *I* | *me* | *my, mine* |
| 2nd person | *you* | *you* | *your* |
| 3rd person | | | |
| masculine | *he* | *him* | *his* |
| feminine | *she* | *her* | *her* |
| neuter | *it* | *it* | *its* |

| **Plural** | | | |
|---|---|---|---|
| 1st person | *we* | *us* | *our, ours* |
| 2nd person | *you* | *you* | *your, yours* |
| 3rd person | *they* | *them* | *their, theirs* |

I took *my* sister to *her* doctor.
They check *their* mailbox more than *I* check *mine*.
His family has *its* favorite holidays; does *yours*?
She gave *us* a new table for *our* kitchen.

An **interrogative** pronoun is used to ask a question. Examples:

*Who* unlocked the car door?
*What* fell out of the tree?
To *whom* did you give the message?
*Whose* book is on the steps?
*Which* is the most expensive perfume?

A **relative** pronoun relates groups of words to nouns or other pronouns. Examples:

Grandpa was the one *who* built the picnic table.
The videotape *that* is now playing is my favorite.
The house, *which* has a garden in bloom, is very inviting.
There are people in the town *whom* I have not met.
I spoke to the child *whose* kitten had climbed the tree.

An **indefinite** pronoun refers to a general, not a specific person or thing. Be sure to use the singular verb form with singular indefinite pronouns.
Singular indefinite pronouns include: *one, each, either, neither, everyone, no one, anybody, somebody, nobody, everybody, anyone, someone.*

*The ESL Teacher's Book of Lists,* © 1993 by John Wiley & Sons, Inc.

*Neither* of the boys wants to have lunch now.

*No one* has a good idea for the bulletin board.

*Everyone* goes to the movies at least once a year.

*Each* of the games takes twelve minutes to play.

Plural indefinite pronouns include: *several, both, many, few.*

*Several* boys want to follow George to the gate.

*Few* were returned because they didn't fit.

*Both* had long brown hair and brown eyes.

*Many* come to the resort to escape the city's noise.

The indefinite pronouns, *some, none, all, most,* and *any,* can be singular or plural depending on the meaning of the sentence.

*Some* of the *marks* come off easily.

*Some* of the *work* is done.

*All* of the *flowers* are dead.

*All* of the *paint* has been scraped off.

A demonstrative pronoun identifies or points out a noun. These are the demonstrative pronouns: *that, this, these, those, such.*

*This* is more fragile than *that.*

*These* are my favorites, not *those.*

I had not seen a jewel *such* as *that* before.

A reflexive pronoun refers to a noun and provides emphasis or shows distinction from others. Reflexive pronouns are formed with the suffixes *-self* and *-selves.*

|  | **Singular** | **Plural** |
|---|---|---|
| 1st person | *myself* | *ourselves* |
| 2nd person | *yourself* | *yourselves* |
| 3rd person | *himself* | *themselves* |
|  | *herself* |  |
|  | *itself* |  |

Mary made the lamp by *herself.*

The boys helped *themselves* to the cookies.

We tried to occupy *ourselves* during the long storm.

# 3-5 YOURS AND MINE:
## Possessive Forms

There are four usual ways to show possession or ownership: possessive pronouns, possessive adjectives, 's, and the words "of" or "belonging to." Example: *His was hanging on the hook. Tom's was hanging on the hook. The one belonging to Tom was hanging on the hook.*

A **possessive pronoun** takes the place of a noun and is an indicator of ownership.

|  | Singular | Plural |
|---|---|---|
| 1st person | *mine* | *ours* |
| 2nd person | *yours* | *yours* |
| 3rd person |  |  |
| masculine | *his* | *theirs* |
| feminine | *hers* | *theirs* |
| neuter | *its* | *theirs* |

*Mine* ran out of ink; may I borrow *yours*?

*Theirs* is parked in the garage; *hers* is at the curb.

*Yours* is still warm; *mine* got cold already.

A **possessive adjective** is used with a noun and indicates ownership. Examples: *my* hat, *our* tickets.

|  | Singular | Plural |
|---|---|---|
| 1st person | *my* | *our* |
| 2nd person | *your* | *your* |
| 3rd person |  |  |
| masculine | *his* | *their* |
| feminine | *her* | *their* |
| neuter | *its* | *their* |

*My* skates are very old; *their* skates are brand new.

*Its* fur was covered with a dusting of snow.

*Our* long-time relationship was based on trust.

Other ways to show possession include adding *'s* after a noun. Add only the apostrophe if the word ends in *-s*. Examples:

| | | |
|---|---|---|
| *Tom's* book | the *picture's* frame | the *class'* teacher |
| *Ann's* desk | the *boss'* phone | the *train's* whistle |

*The ESL Teacher's Book of Lists*, © 1993 by John Wiley & Sons, Inc.

You can also show possession by using the words "of" or "belonging to." Examples:

the mayor *of* the town
the cry *of* the infants
the laughter *of* the children
the temperature *of* the water
the cat *belonging to* Jill
the car *belonging to* the child's father
a ring *belonging to* my grandmother

# 3–6  *LITTLE THINGS MEAN A LOT:*
## *Articles*

**Articles** (also called determiners and noun markers) are adjectives that precede and identify nouns. A **definite article** designates a particular thing; an **indefinite article** designates one of a class of things; and **partitive articles** designate portions of the class.

## DEFINITE ARTICLES

| | | |
|---|---|---|
| singular | *the* | Give me *the* ticket. |
| plural | *the* | Give me *the* tickets. |

## INDEFINITE ARTICLES

| | | |
|---|---|---|
| singular | *a* | I see *a* box. (Use "a" before nouns beginning with all consonants, except "h.") |
| | *an* | I see *an* elephant. (Use "an" before nouns beginning with vowels or the letter "h.") |
| plural | *some* | I see (*some*) boxes.<br>I see (*some*) elephants. |

## PARTITIVE ARTICLES

These partitive articles are used with nouns that can be counted:

| | |
|---|---|
| a few | Jason ate *a few* raisins. |
| some | *Some* toys were left in the playground. |
| a lot of | I could use *a lot of* tickets for my friends. |
| many | Ellen tried *many* recipes for chocolate cake. |

These partitive articles are used with nouns that cannot be counted:

| | |
|---|---|
| a little | I got *a little* sleep between meetings. |
| some | Bring me *some* hot tea, please. |
| a lot of | The cancellation caused *a lot of* trouble. |
| much | There isn't *much* rice left in the pantry. |

# 3–7 AND OR BUT?:
## Conjunctions

**Conjunctions** are used to join words, phrases, and clauses. Conjunctions coordinate equal sentence parts within a sentence, or they subordinate a dependent clause to an independent clause in a sentence.

The ESL Teacher's Book of Lists, © 1993 by John Wiley & Sons, Inc.

| | |
|---|---|
| and | Chris is reading a book, *and* Jenn is writing a letter. |
| but | Nancy wanted to go, *but* Marie did not. |
| for | The students were tired, *for* they had waited for the bus for more than two hours. |
| nor | The cashier should not be blamed for the broken vase, *nor* should we blame the store manager. |
| or | He will finish his report on time, *or* he will not get a good grade in the course. |
| so | We were in a hurry to leave, *so* everyone helped pack the car. |
| still | Computers save businesses a lot of time, *still* it takes weeks to correct an error on a bill. |
| yet | They were happy to graduate, *yet* they knew they would miss this school. |
| consequently | Our team did not have enough members to play yesterday; *consequently*, we had to forfeit the game. |
| furthermore | Classes will be cancelled this afternoon in honor of the President's visit; *furthermore*, a reception will be held at 4 P.M. in Grand Hall. |
| however | No one in the class earned a "B" on the last test; *however*, three students earned "A's." |
| moreover | Sports foster school spirit and cooperation; *moreover*, they develop students' self-esteem. |
| nevertheless | The train was delayed and the taxi got lost; *nevertheless*, Mr. Sidon got to his office on time. |
| therefore | Samantha was finished first; *therefore*, she may choose the next puzzle. |
| after | *After* they read the reviews, the cast went to the party. |
| although | *Although* I heard the song three times a day, I had not tired of it. |
| as if | He walked into the room *as if* nothing had happened. |
| because | Her mother drove her to school *because* the bus drivers were on strike. |
| if | *If* it rains on Saturday, we'll go to the park on Sunday instead. |
| since | *Since* he went on a diet, he lost thirty-two pounds and feels much better about himself. |
| so that | Take the chairs off the stage *so that* we will have enough room for the piano. |
| that | We thought *that* Alicia had baked the cookies. |
| till | *Till* we had the accident, the car had not had engine problems. |
| until | *Until* we fix the leak, we must check the pipes frequently. |

when          *When* it snows, my mother likes to bake bread.

where         Meet me at the restaurant on the corner *where* Main Street
              intersects with Columbus Avenue.

while         *While* I waited for the light to change, I looked at the
              directions and map.

*The ESL Teacher's Book of Lists,* © 1993 by John Wiley & Sons, Inc.

# 3-8  SHORTCUTS:
## Contractions

| | | | |
|---|---|---|---|
| I am | I'm | I have | I've |
| you are | you're | you have | you've |
| he is | he's | he has | he's |
| she is | she's | she has | she's |
| it is | it's | it has | it's |
| we are | we're | we have | we've |
| you are | you're | you have | you've |
| they are | they're | they have | they've |
| | | | |
| what is | what's | what have | what've |
| that is | that's | that have | that've |
| who is | who's | who has | who's |
| who are | who're | who have | who've |
| here is | here's | would have | would've |
| there is | there's | could have | could've |
| | | should have | should've |
| | | might have | might've |
| let us | let's | there have | there've |
| | | | |
| I would | I'd | I had | I'd |
| you would | you'd | you had | you'd |
| she would | she'd | she had | she'd |
| he would | he'd | he had | he'd |
| it would | it'd | it had | it'd |
| we would | we'd | we had | we'd |
| they would | they'd | they had | they'd |
| there would | there'd | there had | there'd |

| who would | who'd | who had | who'd |
|-----------|-------|---------|-------|
| I will | I'll | cannot | can't |
| you will | you'll | do not | don't |
| she will | she'll | will not | won't |
| he will | he'll | is not | isn't |
| it will | it'll | should not | shouldn't |
| we will | we'll | could not | couldn't |
| you will | you'll | would not | wouldn't |
| they will | they'll | are not | aren't |
| that will | that'll | does not | doesn't |
| these will | these'll | was not | wasn't |
| those will | those'll | were not | weren't |
| there will | there'll | has not | hasn't |
| this will | this'll | had not | hadn't |
| what will | what'll | have not | haven't |
| who will | who'll | must not | mustn't |
| | | did not | didn't |
| | | might not | mightn't |
| | | need not | needn't |

# 3–9  NO SOLOS HERE:
## Plurals

A **plural**, the noun form that refers to more than one, is usually formed by adding *-s* to the singular form. If the singular noun ends in *-s, -sh, -ch, -x,* or *-z,* the plural is formed by adding *-es.* Examples:

| | | | |
|---|---|---|---|
| cat | *cats* | dish | *dishes* |
| floor | *floors* | fox | *foxes* |
| cabinet | *cabinets* | waltz | *waltzes* |
| smile | *smiles* | floss | *flosses* |
| disk | *disks* | bench | *benches* |

The plurals of words ending with a consonant followed by *-y* are formed by changing the *-y* to *-i* and adding *-es.* The plurals of words ending with a vowel followed by *-y* are formed by adding *-s.*

| | | | |
|---|---|---|---|
| city | *cities* | valley | *valleys* |
| baby | *babies* | trolley | *trolleys* |
| rally | *rallies* | turkey | *turkeys* |
| lady | *ladies* | alley | *alleys* |
| country | *countries* | key | *keys* |

The plurals of most nouns ending with *-f* or *-fe* are formed by adding *-s;* for some, the plurals are formed by changing the *-f* to *-v* and adding *-es.*

| | | | |
|---|---|---|---|
| gulf | *gulfs* | knife | *knives* |
| chief | *chiefs* | half | *halves* |
| belief | *beliefs* | leaf | *leaves* |
| safe | *safes* | self | *selves* |

The plurals of most nouns ending with *-o* preceded by a consonant are formed by adding *-es.* The plurals of most nouns ending in *-o* preceded by a vowel are formed by adding *-s.*

| | | | |
|---|---|---|---|
| hero | *heroes* | radio | *radios* |
| potato | *potatoes* | studio | *studios* |
| tomato | *tomatoes* | video | *videos* |

The plurals of compound words are formed by making the base noun or second noun plural.

| | |
|---|---|
| brother-in-law | *brothers-in-law* |
| passer-by | *passers-by* |
| bucketseat | *bucketseats* |
| sandbox | *sandboxes* |

These are some nouns that have irregular plural forms:

| | | | |
|---|---|---|---|
| child | *children* | foot | *feet* |
| ox | *oxen* | mouse | *mice* |
| louse | *lice* | radius | *radii* |
| piano | *pianos* | Eskimo | *Eskimos* |
| sheep | *sheep* | tooth | *teeth* |
| trout | *trout* | deer | *deer* |
| salmon | *salmon* | woman | *women* |
| man | *men* | goose | *geese* |
| series | *series* | species | *species* |
| basis | *bases* | stimulus | *stimuli* |
| crisis | *crises* | medium | *media* |
| index | *indices* | criterion | *criteria* |

# 3–10 DOTS AND DASHES:
## Punctuation

There are twelve punctuation marks: apostrophe, colon, comma, dash, ellipsis points, exclamation point, hyphen, parentheses, period, question mark, quotation marks, and semicolon.

Use an **apostrophe** ('):

To show ownership

> *Malik's radio*
> the *Ross' house*

To show the omission of letters in contractions, numbers, or dialect

> *can't*
> *class of '94*
> *ma'am*

To form the plurals of letters, numbers, and symbols

> Cross your *t's*.
> Jorge got three *100's* on his quizzes.
> There are +*'s* and −*'s* in every situation.

Use a **colon** (:):

Before a list or series

> *Hasan ordered his usual: two cheeseburgers, large fries, and a large soda.*

After the greeting in a business letter

> *Dear Sir:*

Between the numerals showing the hour and minutes in time

> *3:45* P.M.

Before a summary or explanatory statement in a complex sentence

> *In short, these were the alternatives: go to the party alone, wait for Anton to pick me up, or go with John.*

Use a **comma** (,):

Between words, phrases, or clauses in a series

> *We need garlic, salt, parsley, pepper, and rosemary.*
> *I like to play the piano, to crochet, and to read.*

The ESL Teacher's Book of Lists, © 1993 by John Wiley & Sons, Inc.

Between a name and a title

*Mary Steward, president*
*Harold Rollins, treasurer*

Between the names of the city and state in an address

*New York, New York*
*Athens, Georgia*

After a noun of direct address

*Adam, where is your brother?*
*David, do you have my keys?*

After "yes" or "no" at the beginning of a sentence

*No, I don't want a sandwich.*
*Yes, I'd like to have lunch now.*

After an introductory phrase

*In summary, the new product has been proven effective.*
*In the meantime, the scouts set up camp near the river.*

Between the day and year in dates

*May 27, 1969*
*March 28, 1972*

Before and after words in apposition

*Jose Marino, the director, spoke to the new employees.*
*Elisa Cortine, the soloist, autographed my program.*

Before and after direct quotations

*He said, "I'm late," as he rushed passed me.*
*"That's not the way I see it," said the young man.*

After the greeting in a friendly letter

*Dear Susan,*
*Dear Mrs. Monaghan,*

After the closing in all letters

*Very truly yours,*
*Sincerely,*

Before the conjunction in a compound sentence

> *The team will play in Denver on Friday, and it will travel to San Francisco on Saturday.*
> *The day was warm and sunny, and there were no clouds in the sky.*

Before the word "too"

> *I want to go, too.*
> *We have chocolate, strawberry, and vanilla, too.*

Between dependent and independent clauses

> *While we waited for the tow truck, we saw the other drive by.*
> *You will have to wait for us, since we can't come sooner.*

Before and after interruptive or explanatory elements in a sentence

> *The bell, for example, is solid brass.*

Before and after contrasting phrases

> *It was Nick, not Chuck, who drove the white car.*
> *The child was found by the cabdriver, not by the firefighter.*

Use a **dash** (—):

Before and after an interruptive element in a sentence

> *I took two—two, mind you, not three—tablets.*

To mark an abrupt change in tone or thought

> *I think I'd like to be—did you see that?*

To mark an incomplete thought or unfinished dialogue

> *I was wondering whether—*

Use **ellipsis points** (...):

To show there are words missing in a direct quotation

> *"The goal of the program...was the development of a new political system."*

Use an **exclamation point** (!):

To mark the end of an exclamatory sentence

> *Happy birthday!*

After an interjection

> *Aha!*

To mark the end of some commands

*Drop that!*

## Use a **hyphen** (-):

Between number and fraction words

*For nearly twenty-five years, the old men met in front of the post office after breakfast.*
*Three-fourths of the class knew the answer.*

At the end of line to divide the last word

*The room was decorated for the celebration.*

Between words in a compound adjective

*The school bought state-of-the-art computers.*

## Use **parentheses** ():

Before and after material that is explanatory or extra

*The living room was large (12' × 26') for an apartment.*

Before and after letters or numbers used in lists

*The directions were simple: (1) trace the design on the wood, (2) cut the wood with a coping saw, and (3) sand the edges smooth.*

## Use a **period** (.):

To mark the end of a statement, command, or request

*The snowplow cleared the road.*
*Turn to the first page of the test.*
*Put the groceries in the pantry, please.*

After initials or abbreviations

*C. S. Lewis*
*Sept.*

In currency and decimal numbers

*$10.00*
*98.6*

After letters and numbers in outlines

*I.*
*1.*
*2.*

*The ESL Teacher's Book of Lists,* © 1993 by John Wiley & Sons, Inc.

*The ESL Teacher's Book of Lists,* © 1993 by John Wiley & Sons, Inc.

Use a **question mark (?)**:

> To mark the end of a question
>
> > *How many books did you read this year?*
>
> To indicate doubt
>
> > *You read two hundred books?*

Use **quotation marks (" ")**:

> Before and after a direct quote
>
> > *Harlan said, "Time is on our side."*
>
> Before and after dialogue
>
> > *"What time would you like to leave?"*
> > *"Oh, at about 5 o'clock, I think."*
>
> Before and after titles of songs, short stories, articles, and poems
>
> > *"Bridge Over Troubled Water"*
> > *"The Open Window"*
>
> Before and after words used in a new or uncertain way
>
> > *"Couch potatoes" are a recent phenomenon.*

Use a **semicolon (;)**:

> Between independent clauses in a compound sentence
>
> > *George had eaten two sandwiches already; he was beginning to feel uncomfortably full.*
>
> Before a conjunction in a complex sentence
>
> > *The president has made his decision; moreover, the senate committee has agreed.*
>
> Between items in a list if they are long or if the items contain commas
>
> > *Nancy took everything she needed: her well-worn, but comfortable shoes; her shopping bag; and, of course, her wallet.*

## 3–11 A CAPITAL IDEA: Capitalization

Use a capital letter for:

The first word of every sentence.

*Margaret Atwood is one of my favorite authors.*
*The car keys are on the table.*

The word I.

*"It's not mine," I said.*
*Joe and I didn't think it was over already.*

All proper nouns.

*The view from the top of the World Trade Center is magnificent.*
*I'd like to go to New Orleans or St. Petersburg for vacation.*
*Jenn studied French and German in high school.*

The names of days, months, and holidays.

*Friday*
*February*
*Fourth of July*

All proper adjectives.

*Members of the British and French governments participated in the flag ceremony.*
*The figs ripened in the bright Californian sun.*

The names of religions, their followers, and important (sacred) religious items.

*Roman Catholic*
*Christians*
*the Bible*
*the Koran*

The names of departments of government.

*Department of Treasury*
*Department of State*

The names of ethnic, social, or other groups.

*The Lenni Lenape tribe lived in New Jersey.*
*Both Democrats and Republicans voted for the tax.*
*Mr. Philips is a member of the Rotary Club.*

The ESL Teacher's Book of Lists, © 1993 by John Wiley & Sons, Inc.

Titles of respect or position.

*Reverend Thomas McCarthy*
*Senator Roger Drummond*
*Superintendent Clementi*

The first word in a quotation.

*The nurse asked, "How long have you had a fever?"*

The first word in lines of most poetry.

*Roses are red,*
*Violets are blue.*

Trade or brand names.

*Kleenex tissues*
*Xerox copy*

The words in a title of a book, newspaper, article, story, **and magazine.**

*The Sun Also Rises*
"Forever Is Composed of Nows"
*The New York Times*
"Economists Predict End of Recession"
*Better Homes and Gardens*

*The ESL Teacher's Book of Lists,* © 1993 by John Wiley & Sons, Inc.

# 3-12  CAN YOU SPELL THAT?:
## Spelling Rules

English orthography, the sound/letter relationships better known as spelling, is a challenge to native and nonnative speakers of the language. Part of its difficulty comes from the fact that many of the words in English are derived from other languages—as many as one-hundred other languages. As a result, English spelling is not as regular as that of a language that has a more limited ancestry. The guidelines here will help you learn the most common patterns of sound/letter relationships.

1.  Before you try to spell a word, say it aloud slowly, one syllable at a time. Listen for the sounds that make up each syllable, then spell the word syllable by syllable.

2.  Every syllable must have one vowel sound. The vowel sound may be spelled with more than one letter. Examples: "Meeting" has two syllables and two vowel sounds—"long e" and an unaccented "short i" or schwa. The vowel sounds are spelled "ee" and "i."

3.  Most consonant sounds have regular, consistent spellings.

| Sound | Spelling | Example |
|-------|----------|---------|
| b | b | *baby* |
| d | d | *dad* |
| f | f | *fat* |
| g | g | *get* |
| h | h | *hat* |
| l | l | *let* |
| m | m | *mom* |
| n | n | *net* |
| p | p | *pin* |
| r | r | *rim* |
| s | s | *sip* |
| t | t | *tap* |
| v | v | *vast* |
| w | w | *web* |
| y | y | *yes* |
| ch | ch | *church* |
| wh | wh | *when* |
| th | th | *thin, that* |
| ng | ng | *ring* |

4.  Some consonant sounds have more than one spelling.

k   Usually spelled "c" if followed by the vowel sounds of "a," "o," or "u." Examples: *cat, cot, cut.* If the sound is at the end of a word, it is often spelled "-ck." Examples: *back, tack, stick.*

f   Usually spelled "f." Sometimes it is spelled "ph" as in *phone, elephant, graph.*

j    Usually spelled "j." If the sound is at the end of word, it is often spelled "-dge" as in *fudge, judge, edge.* If the sound is followed by the vowels "e," "i," or "y," it is spelled with a "g." Examples: *gem, giant, gym.*

s    Usually spelled "s." If the sound is followed by the vowel sounds of "e," "i," or "y," it may be spelled with a "c." Examples: *cent, city, cycle.*

z    Usually spelled "z." Examples: *zoo, ozone, Oz.* It is spelled "s" when it is a voiced plural or inflected ending and sometimes after the letter "o." Examples: *tables, sits, rose.*

sh    Usually spelled "sh." Examples: *shine, fashion, flash.* Sometimes spelled "-ti-," "-si-," or "-ci-" as part of suffixes. Examples: *attention, tension, special.*

5. The short vowel sounds have regular spellings.

| Sound | Spelling | Example |
|---|---|---|
| a | a | *cat* |
| e | e | *let* |
| i | i | *sit* |
| o | o | *cot* |
| u | u | *cut* |

6. The long vowel sounds have several spellings. The spelling used depends on the word's meaning units. Meaning units are prefixes, suffixes, and base words. For example, "long e" may be spelled "e," "ea," "ee," or "-y." In the word "re-turn" it is spelled "e" because it keeps the spelling of the prefix "re."

| Sound | Spelling | Example |
|---|---|---|
| a | a | *acorn* |
|  | ai | *rain* |
|  | ay | *day* |
|  | a _ e | *tame* |
| e | e | *pretense* |
|  | ee | *feet* |
|  | ea | *seat* |
|  | -y | *lucky* |
| i | i | *bicycle* |
|  | i _ e | *ice* |
| o | o | *noble* |
|  | oa | *toast* |
|  | o _ e | *stone* |
|  | ow | *glow* |
| u | u | *universe* |
|  | u _ e | *tune* |

7. The vowels in unaccented syllables are sounded as schwas but keep the spelling of their meaning units. Example: The word *portable* is made of the base word *port* meaning "to carry" and the suffix *able* meaning "able to be."

The *a* is in an unaccented syllable and is pronounced as a schwa; however, it is part of *-able* and keeps the spelling of the suffix.

8. *ie* is more common than *ei.* This well-known rhyme is a good guide:

> Use *i* before *e,*
> Except after *c,*
> Or when sounded like *a,*
> As in *neighbor* and *weigh.*

Exceptions you need to learn:

| | | | |
|---|---|---|---|
| agencies | ancient | conscience | counterfeit |
| either | efficient | deity | Fahrenheit |
| fancier | financier | foreign | forfeit |
| height | kaleidoscope | leisure | neither |
| protein | proficient | science | seismograph |
| seize | sheik | society | sovereign |
| species | weird | | |

9. When adding a suffix that begins with a vowel to a base word that ends in "e," drop the "e" before adding the suffix. If the suffix begins with a consonant, keep the final "e" on the base word. Examples:

| | | | |
|---|---|---|---|
| love | + | ing | = | *loving* |
| love | + | ly | = | *lovely* |

10. If a base word ends with a vowel followed by a consonant (-vc), double the consonant before adding a suffix that begins with a vowel (-vccv-). Don't double the consonant before a suffix that begins with a consonant (-vcc-). Examples:

| | | | | | |
|---|---|---|---|---|---|
| tan | + | ed | = | *tanned* | (vccv-) |
| dim | + | er | = | *dimmer* | (vccv-) |
| dim | + | ly | = | *dimly* | (vcc-) |
| commit | + | ed | = | *committed* | (vccv-) |
| commit | + | ment | = | *commitment* | (vccv--) |

11. Common prefixes you should learn to spell:

| Prefix | Meaning | Example |
|---|---|---|
| anti- | against | *antiwar* |
| auto- | self | *autobiography* |
| bi- | two | *bicycle* |
| cent- | hundred | *century* |
| inter- | between | *interstate* |
| mid- | middle | *midstream* |
| poly- | many | *polyglot* |
| pre- | before | *predict* |
| re- | again | *rerun* |
| sub- | under | *submarine* |

*The ESL Teacher's Book of Lists,* © 1993 by John Wiley & Sons, Inc.

| | | |
|---|---|---|
| ultra- | beyond | *ultraconservative* |
| un- | not | *unclear* |
| under- | below | *underground* |

12. Common suffixes you should learn to spell:

| **Suffix** | **Meaning** | **Example** |
|---|---|---|
| -ist | one who | *artist* |
| -or | one who | *actor* |
| -hood | state of | *childhood* |
| -ation | process of | *computation* |
| -ology | study of | *biology* |
| -less | without | *careless* |
| -ful | full of | *fearful* |
| -en | made of | *wooden* |
| -ical | relating to | *hysterical* |
| -ate | to make | *activate* |
| -able | able to be | *washable* |

*The ESL Teacher's Book of Lists,* © 1993 by John Wiley & Sons, Inc.

# 3–13 YESTERDAY, TODAY, AND TOMORROW: Verbs

Verbs show physical or mental action or the state of being of a subject. For example, *sit, think, swim, breathe, appear* and *know* are all verbs. Verbs have different forms to show person, voice, tense, and mood.

**Person**

Person relates to the subject of the verb. It can be first, second, or third person, singular or plural. Verbs use different endings and forms to show person.

**Voice**

A verb is in the active voice when the subject is the agent or doer of the action. A verb is in the passive voice when the subject is the receiver of the action.

EXAMPLES:
Active  *Marie baked the pie.*
Passive  *The pie was baked by Marie.*

**Tense**

Verb tense shows the time of the action. The simple tenses are the present, the past, and the future. The perfect tenses are the present perfect, past perfect, and future perfect. The progressive tenses are the present progressive, present perfect progressive, past perfect progressive, and future perfect progressive.

**Mood**

Verb moods help to show the intention of the speaker or writer. The moods are indicative, imperative, and subjunctive.

The indicative mood is used to make statements or ask questions.

EXAMPLES: *I baked an apple pie. Where did you get that hat?*

The imperative mood is used for commands or requests.

EXAMPLES: *Wash your hands. Please go to the store.*

The subjunctive mood is used to express a wish, a condition contrary to fact, or a request.

EXAMPLES: *I wish I were taller. If I begin this project, will you finish it for me? If I had dealt you another card, would you have won?*

**Verb parts**

There are five principal parts of a verb:

|  | Regular verb | Irregular verb |
| --- | --- | --- |
| Infinitive | to mend | to go |
| Present | mend | go |
| Present participle | mending | going |
| Past | mended | went |
| Past participle | mended | gone |

*The ESL Teacher's Book of Lists,* © 1993 by John Wiley & Sons, Inc.

**Regular verb**    A regular verb forms its past tense and past participle by adding -d or -ed to the verb base.

EXAMPLES: *look, looked, looked; thank, thanked, thanked.*

**Irregular verb**    An irregular verb does not form its past tense and past participle by adding -d or -ed to the verb base. Its past and past participle forms do not follow a pattern and must be learned.

| Present | Past | Past Participle | Present | Past | Past Participle |
|---------|------|-----------------|---------|------|-----------------|
| awake | awoke | awakened | beat | beat | beaten |
| begin | began | begun | bite | bit | bitten |
| blow | blew | blown | break | broke | broken |
| bring | brought | brought | build | built | built |
| buy | bought | bought | catch | caught | caught |
| cut | cut | cut | do | did | done |
| drink | drank | drunk | drive | drove | driven |
| eat | ate | eaten | fall | fell | fallen |
| fight | fought | fought | find | found | found |
| fly | flew | flown | forget | forgot | forgotten |
| forgive | forgave | forgiven | freeze | froze | frozen |
| get | got | got | give | gave | given |
| go | went | gone | grow | grew | grown |
| have | had | had | hear | heard | heard |
| hold | held | held | know | knew | known |
| leave | left | left | make | made | made |
| meet | met | met | ride | rode | ridden |
| ring | rang | rung | run | ran | run |
| say | said | said | see | saw | seen |
| sell | sold | sold | send | sent | sent |
| sing | sang | sung | sink | sank | sunk |
| sit | sat | sat | sleep | slept | slept |
| speak | spoke | spoken | take | took | taken |
| teach | taught | taught | tear | tore | torn |
| think | thought | thought | wear | wore | worn |
| win | won | won | write | wrote | written |

The verb *to be* is a special case. It also has irregular present forms:

| | |
|---|---|
| present | *am, are, is* |
| past | *was* |
| past participle | *been* |

**Auxiliary verb**    An auxiliary verb is used with the main verb to help clarify the grammar or meaning in a sentence.

Modal auxiliary verbs convey meaning. They help to show obligations, abilities, desires, permissions, requests, possibilities, or viewpoints. These are modal auxiliary verbs:

| | | |
|---|---|---|
| *be able* | *be supposed to* | *can* |
| *could* | *had better* | *have got to* |
| *have to* | *may* | *might* |
| *must* | *ought to* | *shall* |
| *should* | *will* | *would* |

Nonmodal auxiliary verbs have grammatical uses. They help to form the different tenses. These are the nonmodal auxiliary verbs:

| | | |
|---|---|---|
| *be* | *have* | *do* |

**Verb conjugation**

To conjugate a verb is to write or say its *forms* for each person, number, tense, and mood.

EXAMPLE: *to cover*    Principle parts of the verb:
*to cover, cover, covering, covered, covered*

## ACTIVE VOICE—INDICATIVE MOOD

| Tense | Singular | Plural |
|---|---|---|
| Present | I cover<br>you cover<br>he covers<br>she covers<br>it covers | we cover<br>you cover<br>they cover |
| Present progressive | I am covering<br>you are covering<br>he is covering<br>she is covering<br>it is covering | we are covering<br>you are covering<br>they are covering |
| Past | I covered<br>you covered<br>he covered<br>she covered<br>it covered | we covered<br>you covered<br>they covered |
| Past progressive | I was covering<br>you were covering<br>he was covering<br>she was covering<br>it was covering | we were covering<br>you were covering<br>they were covering |

*The ESL Teacher's Book of Lists,* © 1993 by John Wiley & Sons, Inc.

| Tense | Singular | Plural |
|---|---|---|
| Future | I will cover<br>you will cover<br>he will cover<br>she will cover<br>it will cover | we will cover<br>you will cover<br>they will cover |
| Future progressive | I will be covering<br>you will be covering<br>he will be covering<br>she will be covering<br>it will be covering | we will be covering<br>you will be covering<br>they will be covering |
| Present perfect | I have covered<br>you have covered<br>he has covered<br>she has covered<br>it has covered | we have covered<br>you have covered<br>they have covered |
| Present perfect progressive | I have been covering<br>you have been covering<br>he has been covering<br>she has been covering<br>it has been covering | we have been covering<br>you have been covering<br>they have been covering |
| Past perfect | I had covered<br>you had covered<br>he had covered<br>she had covered<br>it had covered | we had covered<br>you had covered<br>they had covered |
| Past perfect progressive | I had been covering<br>you had been covering<br>he had been covering<br>she had been covering<br>it had been covering | we had been covering<br>you had been covering<br>they had been covering |
| Future perfect | I will have covered<br>you will have covered<br>he will have covered<br>she will have covered<br>it will have covered | we will have covered<br>you will have covered<br>they will have covered |
| Future perfect progressive | I will have been covering<br>you will have been covering<br>he will have been covering<br>she will have been covering<br>it will have been covering | we will have been covering<br>you will have been covering<br>they will have been covering |

| Tense | Singular | Plural |
|---|---|---|
| Conditional | I would cover<br>you would cover<br>he would cover<br>she would cover<br>it would cover | we would cover<br>you would cover<br>they would cover |
| Conditional progressive | I would be covering<br>you would be covering<br>he would be covering<br>she would be covering<br>it would be covering | we would be covering<br>you would be covering<br>they would be covering |
| Conditional perfect | I would have covered<br>you would have covered<br>he would have covered<br>she would have covered | we would have covered<br>you would have covered<br>they would have covered |
| Conditional perfect progressive | I would have been covering<br>you would have been covering<br>he would have been covering<br>she would have been covering<br>it would have been covering | we would have been covering<br>you would have been covering<br>they would have been covering |

## ACTIVE VOICE—IMPERATIVE MOOD

| Singular | Plural |
|---|---|
| cover | cover |

## ACTIVE VOICE—SUBJUNCTIVE MOOD

| Tense | Singular | Plural |
|---|---|---|
| Present | if I cover<br>if you cover<br>if he covers<br>if she covers<br>if it covers | if we cover<br>if you cover<br>if they cover |
| Past | if I covered<br>if you covered<br>if he covered<br>if she covered<br>if it covered | if we covered<br>if you covered<br>if they covered |

*The ESL Teacher's Book of Lists,* © 1993 by John Wiley & Sons, Inc.

*The ESL Teacher's Book of Lists,* © 1993 by John Wiley & Sons, Inc.

| Tense | Singular | Plural |
|---|---|---|
| Future | if I should cover<br>if you should cover<br>if he should cover<br>if she should cover<br>if it should cover | if we should cover<br>if you should cover<br>if they should cover |

## PASSIVE VOICE—INDICATIVE MOOD

| Tense | Singular | Plural |
|---|---|---|
| Present | I am covered<br>you are covered<br>he is covered<br>she is covered<br>it is covered | we are covered<br>you are covered<br>they are covered |
| Present progressive | I am being covered<br>you are being covered<br>he is being covered<br>she is being covered<br>it is being covered | we are being covered<br>you are being covered<br>they are being covered |
| Past | I was covered<br>you were covered<br>he was covered<br>she was covered<br>it was covered | we were covered<br>you were covered<br>they were covered |
| Past progressive | I was being covered<br>you were being covered<br>he was being covered<br>she was being covered<br>it was being covered | we were being covered<br>you were being covered<br>they were being covered |
| Future | I will be covered<br>you will be covered<br>he will be covered<br>she will be covered<br>it will be covered | we will be covered<br>you will be covered<br>they will be covered |
| Present perfect | I have been covered<br>you have been covered<br>he has been covered<br>she has been covered<br>it has been covered | we have been covered<br>you have been covered<br>they have been covered |
| Past perfect | I had been covered<br>you had been covered<br>he had been covered<br>she had been covered<br>it had been covered | we had been covered<br>you had been covered<br>they had been covered |

| Tense | Singular | Plural |
|---|---|---|
| Future perfect | I will have been covered<br>you will have been covered<br>he will have been covered<br>she will have been covered | we will have been covered<br>you will have been covered<br>they will have been covered |

## PASSIVE—IMPERATIVE MOOD

| Singular | Plural |
|---|---|
| be covered | be covered |

## PASSIVE VOICE—SUBJUNCTIVE MOOD

| | Singular | Plural |
|---|---|---|
| Present | if I be covered<br>if you be covered<br>if he be covered<br>if she be covered<br>if it be covered | if we be covered<br>if you be covered<br>if they be covered |
| Past | if I were covered<br>if you were covered<br>if he was covered<br>if she was covered<br>if he was covered | if we were covered<br>if you were covered<br>if they were covered |
| Future | if I should be covered<br>if you should be covered<br>if he should be covered<br>if she should be covered<br>if it should be covered | if we should be covered<br>if you should be covered<br>if they should be covered |

*The ESL Teacher's Book of Lists,* © 1993 by John Wiley & Sons, Inc.

# SECTION 4

# Grammar Patterns and Practice

# 4–1  *BASIC SENTENCE PATTERNS*

## SIMPLE PATTERNS

**N/V**  **noun/verb**

The boys/ran.
Four women/sewed.
The faucet/dripped.
A balloon/burst.
Children/laughed.

**N/V/AD**  **noun/verb/adverb**

The glass/broke/suddenly.
I/drove/home.
We/left/early in the morning.
Richard/trained/all season.
Annette/typed/furiously.

**N/V/N**  **noun/verb/noun**

The carpenter/built/the bookcase.
The artist/painted/the picture.
The choir/sings/hymns.
An elephant/eats/peanuts.
The cat/caught/a mouse.

**N/V/N/N**  **noun/verb/noun/noun**

Mom/made/Jennifer/an afghan.
Christine/bought/her/flowers.
Jackie/gave/them/tickets.
The representatives/elected/Duncan/chairman.
Sid/called/Mary/a cab.

**N/V/N/ADJ**  **noun/verb/noun/adjective**

We/found/the door/open.
You/are driving/me/crazy.
She/served/the soup/cold.
They/painted/the deck/green.
The frosting/made/the cake/fattening.

**N/LV/N**  **noun/linking verb/noun**

David/is/an officer.
The party/will be/a surprise.
The owner/was/a musician.
The desk/could have been/an antique.
The drivers/were/professionals.

**N/LV/ADJ**   **noun/linking verb/adjective**

Love/is/grand.
Julia/seems/tired.
The apples/were/tart.
Norman/feels/ill.
The potatoes/tasted/salty.

## COMPOUND PATTERNS

**N/V**   **noun/verb**

Tom and Harry/studied.
The roses and begonias/bloomed.
The old lady/complained and complained.
The tigers/roared and attacked.
The mother and child/watched and smiled.
Emma and Joan/sang and danced.

**N/V/AD**   **noun/verb/adverb**

The books and papers/were scattered/on the desk.
Your letter and package/arrived/yesterday.
She/typed and filed/expertly.
They/designed and painted/carefully.
The thief/entered/slowly and noiselessly.
The guests/gathered/on the deck and in the house.

**N/V/N**   **noun/verb/noun**

The principal and teachers/greeted/the students.
Hydrogen and oxygen/form/water.
Jason/sorted and stacked/his baseball cards.
Christopher/picked and arranged/his chessmen.
Lisa/carried/her doll and teddy bear.
Adam/wore/a jacket and hat.

**N/V/N/N**   **noun/verb/noun/noun**

Ryan and Dave/gave/Gerry/a watch.
Chuck/planned and built/Alicia/a dollhouse.
Kathy/gave/Jackie and Gloria/Christmas presents.
Nick/cooked/Camille/shrimp and scallops.

**N/V/N/ADJ**   **noun/verb/noun/adjective**

The heat and humidity/made/Mike/tired.
The judge/thought and called/the winner/exceptional.
The surprise/made/Darin and Samantha/happy.
Phil/found/Gloria/interesting and beautiful.

*The ESL Teacher's Book of Lists,* © 1993 by John Wiley & Sons, Inc.

**N/LV/N**        **noun/linking verb/noun**

Washington and Jefferson/were/presidents.
You/can and will be/a winner.
John/is/a skier and sailor.

**N/LV/ADJ**        **noun/linking verb/adjective**

The coffee and tea/were/hot.
Reading/is and will be/necessary.
The model/is/tall and slender.

*The ESL Teacher's Book of Lists*, © 1993 by John Wiley & Sons, Inc.

# 4–2  SENTENCE PATTERNS USING TO BE

**Present Tense**

I am hungry.
I'm hungry.
You are hungry.
You're hungry.

He is hungry.
He's hungry.

She is hungry.
She's hungry.

It is hungry.
It's hungry.

We are hungry.
We're hungry.

You are hungry.
You're hungry.

They are hungry.
They're hungry.

It is time to go.
It's time to go.
There is time to spare.
There's time to spare.
This is the car.
These are the cars.

**Past Tense**

I was hungry.

You were hungry.

He was hungry.

She was hungry.

It was hungry.

I am not hungry.
I'm not hungry.
You are not hungry.
You aren't hungry.
You're not hungry.
He is not hungry.
He isn't hungry.
He's not hungry.
She is not hungry.
She isn't hungry.
She's not hungry.
It is not hungry.
It isn't hungry.
It's not hungry.

We are not hungry.
We aren't hungry.
We're not hungry.

You are not hungry.
You aren't hungry.
You're not hungry.

They are not hungry.
They aren't hungry.
They're not hungry.

It isn't time to go.
It's not time to go.
There isn't time to spare.
There's no time to spare.
This isn't the car.
These aren't the cars.

I was not hungry.
I wasn't hungry.
You were not hungry.
You weren't hungry.
He was not hungry.
He wasn't hungry.
She was not hungry.
She wasn't hungry.
It was not hungry.
It wasn't hungry.

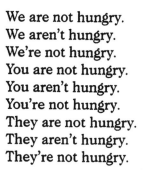

*The ESL Teacher's Book of Lists*, © 1993 by John Wiley & Sons, Inc.

### Past Tense (*continued*)

| | |
|---|---|
| We were hungry. | We were not hungry. |
| | We weren't hungry. |
| You were hungry. | You were not hungry. |
| | You weren't hungry. |
| They were hungry. | They were not hungry. |
| | They weren't hungry. |
| | |
| It was time to go. | It wasn't time to go. |
| There was time to spare. | There wasn't time to spare. |
| | There was no time to spare. |
| | |
| This was the car. | This wasn't the car. |
| These were the cars. | These weren't the cars. |

### Future Tense

| | |
|---|---|
| I will be . . . | I will not be . . . |
| I'll be . . . | I won't be . . . |
| You will be . . . | You will not be . . . |
| You'll be . . . | You won't be . . . |
| He will be . . . | He will not be . . . |
| He'll be . . . | He won't be . . . |
| She will be . . . | She will not be . . . |
| She'll be . . . | She won't be . . . |
| It will be . . . | It will not be . . . |
| It'll be . . . | It won't be . . . |
| | |
| We will be . . . | We will not be . . . |
| We'll be . . . | We won't be . . . |
| You will be . . . | You will not be . . . |
| You'll be . . . | You won't be . . . |
| They will be . . . | They will not be . . . |
| They'll be . . . | They won't be . . . |
| | |
| This will be . . . | This will not be . . . |
| This'll be . . . | This won't be . . . |
| These will be . . . | These will not be . . . |
| These'll be . . . | These won't be . . . |
| There will be . . . | There will not be . . . |
| There'll be . . . | There won't be . . . |

### Present Perfect Tense

| | |
|---|---|
| I have been . . . | I have not been . . . |
| I've been . . . | I haven't been . . . |
| You have been . . . | You have not been . . . |
| You've been . . . | You haven't been . . . |
| He has been . . . | He has not been . . . |
| He's been . . . | He hasn't been . . . |
| She has been . . . | She has not been . . . |
| She's been . . . | She hasn't been . . . |

**Present Perfect Tense (*continued*)**

| | |
|---|---|
| It has been . . . | It has not been . . . |
| It's been . . . | It hasn't been . . . |
| We have been . . . | We have not been . . . |
| We've been . . . | We haven't been . . . |
| You have been . . . | You have not been . . . |
| You've been . . . | You haven't been . . . |
| They have been . . . | They have not been . . . |
| They've been . . . | They haven't been . . . |

| | |
|---|---|
| This has been . . . | This has not been . . . |
| This's been . . . | This hasn't been . . . |
| These have been . . . | These have not been . . . |
| These've been . . . | These haven't been . . . |
| There has been . . . | There has not been . . . |
| There's been . . . | There hasn't been . . . |

**Past Perfect Tense**

| | |
|---|---|
| I had been . . . | I had not been . . . |
| I'd been . . . | I hadn't been . . . |
| You had been . . . | You had not been . . . |
| You'd been . . . | You hadn't been . . . |
| He had been . . . | He had not been . . . |
| He'd been . . . | He hadn't been . . . |
| She had been . . . | She had not been . . . |
| She'd been . . . | She hadn't been . . . |
| It had been . . . | It had not been . . . |
| It'd been . . . | It hadn't been . . . |

| | |
|---|---|
| We had been . . . | We had not been . . . |
| We'd been . . . | We hadn't been . . . |
| You had been . . . | You had not been . . . |
| You'd been . . . | You hadn't been . . . |
| They had been . . . | They had not been . . . |
| They'd been . . . | They hadn't been . . . |

| | |
|---|---|
| This had been . . . | This had not been . . . |
| This'd been . . . | This hadn't been . . . |
| These had been . . . | These had not been . . . |
| These'd been . . . | These hadn't been . . . |
| There had been . . . | There had not been . . . |
| There'd been . . . | There hadn't been . . . |

**Future Perfect Tense**

| | |
|---|---|
| I shall have been . . . | I shall not have been . . . |
| I'll have been . . . | I shan't have been . . . |
| You will have been . . . | You will not have been . . . |
| You'll have been . . . | You won't have been . . . |
| He will have been . . . | He will not have been . . . |

*The ESL Teacher's Book of Lists*, © 1993 by John Wiley & Sons, Inc.

**Future Perfect Tense (*continued*)**

| | |
|---|---|
| He'll have been . . . | He won't have been . . . |
| She will have been . . . | She will not have been . . . |
| She'll have been . . . | She won't have been . . . |
| It will have been . . . | It will not have been . . . |
| It'll have been . . . | It won't have been . . . |

| | |
|---|---|
| We shall have been . . . | We shall not have been . . . |
| We'll have been . . . | We shall not have been . . . |
| You will have been . . . | You will not have been . . . |
| You'll have been . . . | You won't have been . . . |
| They will have been . . . | They will not have been . . . |
| They'll have been . . . | They won't have been . . . |

| | |
|---|---|
| This will have been . . . | This will not have been . . . |
| This'll have been . . . | This won't have been . . . |
| These will have been . . . | These will not have been . . . |
| These'll have been . . . | These won't have been . . . |
| There will have been . . . | There will not have been . . . |
| There'll have been . . . | There won't have been . . . |

# 4–3 NEGATIVE SENTENCE PATTERNS

There are three usual ways to express negation in English: negate the verb in the sentence, negate a noun in the sentence, or use a special negative word.

## NEGATING THE VERB

To negate the verb in a sentence, add "not" between the auxiliary and the main verb. If the verb does not have an auxiliary, use its emphatic transformation and the auxiliary "do" or "does." Contractions are frequently used in negative sentences. Examples:

| Positive | Transformation | Negative |
|---|---|---|
| I see it. | I do see it. | *I do not see it.* |
| | | *I don't see it.* |
| I have it. | I do have it. | *I do not have it.* |
| | | *I don't have it.* |
| He carries them. | He does carry them. | *He does not carry them.* |
| | | *He doesn't carry them.* |
| I saw it. | I did see it. | *I did not see it.* |
| | | *I didn't see it.* |
| He could fix the tire. | | *He could not fix the tire.* |
| | | *He couldn't fix the tire.* |
| I will go to the store. | | *I will not go to the store.* |
| | | *I won't go to the store.* |
| We were going swimming. | | *We were not going swimming.* |
| | | *We weren't going swimming.* |
| It is time to go. | | *It is not time to go.* |
| | | *It isn't time to go.* |

*The ESL Teacher's Book of Lists,* © 1993 by John Wiley & Sons, Inc.

## NEGATING A NOUN

To negate a noun, add "no" before the noun. Examples:

| | |
|---|---|
| We have time to spare. | *We have no time to spare.* |
| I found money in the park. | *I found no money in the park.* |
| Photographs were taken Friday. | *No photographs were taken Friday.* |

## USING A SPECIAL NEGATIVE WORD

These words are also used to express negation: nobody, nothing, nowhere, none, no one, and neither/nor. Examples:

*Nobody found Angela's wallet.*

*There was nothing left in the jar.*

*Nowhere else is more beautiful than this valley.*

*None of the common names suited the puppy.*

*No one knew how to turn off the generator.*

*Neither Allen nor Bill told Frankie the score.*

# 4-4 SENTENCE PATTERNS FOR QUESTIONS AND ANSWERS

## USING QUESTION WORDS

Who called the taxi?

Mary.
Mary called.
Mary called it.
Mary called the taxi.

Who is waiting?
Who's waiting?

Harry.
Harry is.
Harry is waiting.

What is in the box?
What's in the box?

A vase.
A vase is.
A vase is in the box.

Where are you going?
Where're you going?

The store.
To the store.
I'm going to the store.

When are you leaving?

In an hour.
I'm leaving in an hour.

Why did he call?
Why'd he call?

To get the answer.
He called to get the answer.

How much does it cost?

Three dollars.
It costs three dollars.

## USING INVERTED WORD ORDER

| | | |
|---|---|---|
| Are you tired? | Yes, I am. | No, I'm not. |
| Aren't you tired? | Yes, I am. | No, I'm not. |
| Is he hungry? | Yes, he is. | No, he's not. |
| Isn't he hungry? | Yes, he is. | No, he isn't. |
| Is it time to go? | Yes, it is. | No, it's not. |
| Isn't it time to go? | Yes, it is. | No, it isn't. |
| Will you be going? | Yes, I will. | No, I won't. |
| Won't you be going? | Yes, I will. | No, I won't. |
| Have you had a cold? | Yes, I have. | No, I haven't. |
| Haven't you had a cold? | Yes, I have. | No, I haven't. |

## USING EMPHATIC OR REQUEST WORDS

| | | |
|---|---|---|
| Did it fall? | Yes, it did. | No, it didn't. |
| Do you like it? | Yes, I do. | No, I don't. |
| Does he have one? | Yes, he does. | No, he doesn't. |
| May I have some? | Yes, you may. | No, you may not. |
| Can we leave? | Yes, we can. | No, we can't. |
| Should I speak? | Yes, you should. | No, you shouldn't. |
| Have they gone? | Yes, they have. | No, they haven't. |
| Has she finished? | Yes, she has. | No, she hasn't. |
| Would you take this? | Yes, I would. | No, I wouldn't. |

## USING TAG QUESTIONS

*The ESL Teacher's Book of Lists,* © 1993 by John Wiley & Sons, Inc.

| | |
|---|---|
| I'm on next, aren't I? | I'm not on next, am I? |
| You're tall, aren't you? | You're not tall, are you? |
| She's busy, isn't she? | She's not busy, is she? |
| It's over, isn't it? | It's not over, is it? |
| We're young, aren't we? | We're not young, are we? |
| They're smiling, aren't they? | They're not smiling, are they? |
| | |
| I was hungry, wasn't I? | I wasn't hungry, was I? |
| You were ill, weren't you? | You weren't ill, were you? |
| He was broke, wasn't he? | He wasn't broke, was he? |
| We were silly, weren't we? | We weren't silly, were we? |
| They were Irish, weren't they? | They weren't Irish, were they? |
| | |
| You'll go, won't you? | You won't go, will you? |
| They'll go, won't they? | They won't go, will they? |
| She can go, can't she? | She can't go, can she? |
| We can go, can't we? | We can't go, can we? |
| | |
| They do know, don't they? | They don't know, do they? |
| She did write, didn't she? | She didn't write, did she? |
| It looks good, doesn't it? | It doesn't look good, does it? |
| The jet has landed, hasn't it? | The jet hasn't landed, has it? |
| He had won, hadn't he? | He hadn't won, had he? |
| I have missed, haven't I? | I haven't missed, have I? |
| | |
| I could do it, couldn't I? | I couldn't do it, could I? |
| They would do it, wouldn't they? | They wouldn't do it, would they? |
| We should do it, shouldn't we? | We shouldn't do it, should we? |

## CLOSED QUESTIONS—YES OR NO ANSWERS

Does Rob like ice cream?
Doesn't Rob like ice cream?
Rob likes ice cream, doesn't he?

## OPEN QUESTIONS—VARIOUS ANSWERS POSSIBLE

What does Rob like?
What doesn't Rob like?

# 4–5 ACTIVE/PASSIVE SENTENCE PATTERNS

The verb in a sentence is in the **active** voice when the subject is the **doer** or agent of the action. The verb is in the **passive** voice when the subject is the **receiver** of the action. The doer or agent of the action is not always stated in a passive sentence.

| **Active** | **Passive** |
|---|---|
| Anthony broke the window. | The window was broken by Anthony. |
| | The window was broken. |
| | |
| A neighbor is watching her. | She is being watched by a neighbor. |
| I am not considering the costs. | The costs are not being considered. |
| He is stirring the soup. | The soup is being stirred by him. |
| The music excites me. | I am excited by the music. |
| Librarians order books. | Books are ordered by librarians. |
| We make decisions daily. | Decisions are made daily. |
| Farmers grow grain. | Grain is grown by farmers. |
| They do not trade jobs often. | Jobs were not traded often by them. |
| She usually makes the tea. | The tea is usually made by her. |
| | |
| Someone stole the car. | The car was stolen. |
| They voted Dawn treasurer. | Dawn was voted treasurer. |
| Sissy gave Jake a watch. | Jake was given a watch by Sissy. |
| Jose did not paint the house. | The house was not painted by Jose. |
| Ellen slammed the door shut. | The door was slammed shut. |
| The boys didn't rake the leaves. | The leaves weren't raked by the boys. |
| The teacher graded the tests. | The tests were graded. |
| Congress raised the taxes. | The taxes were raised by Congress. |
| Phil drank the soda. | The soda was drunk by Phil. |
| | |
| Jill will not call Rosa. | Rosa will not be called by Jill. |
| Harry will fix the VCR. | The VCR will be fixed. |
| They will break the record. | The record will be broken by them. |
| We will bring the boxes. | The boxes will be brought by us. |
| Andy will tease Annette. | Annette will be teased by Andy. |
| I will operate the machine. | The machine will be operated by me. |
| Ed will appoint the captain. | The captain will be appointed by Ed. |
| I will not do it. | It will not be done by me. |
| Someone will take us. | We will be taken by someone. |

# 4–6  SUBJECT-VERB AGREEMENT

For subject-verb agreement, use the singular verb form with a singular subject and the plural verb form with a plural subject. Examples:

Singular    *The box is on the table.*
Plural    *The boxes are on the table.*

Singular    *I was packing my suitcase when he called.*
Plural    *We were packing our suitcases when he called.*

Singular    *That artist paints well.*
Plural    *Those artists paint well.*

Compound subjects refer to more than one doer or agent of the action in the sentence and, therefore, they need plural verbs. Examples:

*The driver checks the truck every night.*
*The driver and mechanic check the truck every night.*

*Joss is asleep in the family room.*
*Joss and Romeo are asleep in the family room.*

*Thunder frightens many people.*
*Thunder and lightning frighten many people.*

These indefinite pronouns are singular and take singular verbs: anybody, anyone, each, either, everybody, everyone, neither, nobody, no one, one, somebody, someone. Examples:

*Is anybody home?*
*Anyone may apply for the scholarship.*
*Of the five models, each has a special feature.*
*Either Rose or Sharon has the list.*
*Everybody needs a dream.*
*Nobody answers the phone after six o'clock.*
*Somebody has to fix the flat tire.*
*Someone is peering in the window.*

These indefinite pronouns are plural and take plural verbs: several, both, many, few. Examples:

*Several of the applicants are waiting in the hall.*
*Both are interested in taking economics courses.*
*Many are not in favor of the new parking regulations.*
*Few of the students returned to the dorm before noon.*

These indefinite pronouns can be singular or plural depending on the meaning of the sentence: some, none, all, most, any. Use a singular verb form if the pronoun refers to a single quantity and use a plural verb if the pronoun refers to more than one unit of something. Examples:

*Some of the work is very difficult.*
*Some of the cookies are burned.*

*All of the coffee has been drunk.*
*All of the tickets have been turned in.*

*Most of the food is in the refrigerator.*
*Most of the choir members are on the bus.*

There is a useful test to determine whether to use the singular or plural verb form. Substitute "he," "it," and "they" for the subject in the sentence. If "he" or "it" makes sense, the subject is singular and takes a singular verb; if "they" makes sense, the subject is plural and takes a plural verb.

Sometimes the subject and verb are separated by adjectives, adverbs, phrases, and even clauses. Don't be confused by the intervening words. Isolate the subject and verb and apply the rules of agreement. Examples:

*Each of the bridges and tunnels in the counties of Cambria and Tuxedo is painted gray.*

*The girl's parents, as well as the high school principal, were anxious to hear what happened at the tournament.*

# 4–7  *TIME AGREEMENT*

Time agreement refers to the consistent use of a tense in a spoken or written sentence, paragraph, or other unit of communication. Examples:

CORRECT:

During the show, Roger *slept*, Tim *whispered* to Joshua, Ann *made* notes, and Alice *took* photographs.

Next week, the band *will record* a new song, their agent *will set* up interviews and the writer *will begin* a biography of the band leader.

INCORRECT:

Last semester we *studied* hard, *read* lots of books and *wonder* who got an A on each test.

CORRECTED:

Last semester we *studied* hard, *read* lots of books and *wondered* who got an A on each test.

INCORRECT:

We *will visit* the museum on Friday. Once there we *have* to keep to our tight schedule or *miss* the train home.

CORRECTED:

We *will visit* the museum on Friday. Once there we *will have* to keep to our tight schedule or we *will miss* the train home.

## PERMITTED TENSE SHIFTS

Sometimes the sentence tells about an event that happened before or will happen after the time of the main action in the sentence. To show this change in time, different tenses are used. Examples:

| | |
|---|---|
| **Same time** | The man *told* us that the boat *was destroyed*. (Both events, the telling and the destroying, happened in the past.) |
| | On Friday, we *will know* what John *will do*. (Both events, the knowing and the doing, will happen in the future.) |
| **Before** | The man *told* us that the boat *had been destroyed* ten years ago. (The destruction of the boat happened before the man told about it.) |
| | We *know* what John *did*. (John's action happened before the knowing.) |
| **After** | The man *told* us that the boat *will be destroyed* next summer. |

(The destruction is expected to occur after the telling about the boat.)

We *know* what John *will do.* (John's action is expected to occur after the knowing.)

# 4–8  COMMON GRAMMATICAL ERRORS

Very often the words **mistake** and **error** are used interchangeably to label something that differs from the accepted standard. In language instruction, mistakes and errors should be differentiated.

Use the word **mistake** when the student produces a spoken or written form that differs from a standard the student knows. For example, the misspelling of a word that the student has learned previously is a mistake. Its correction is a matter for proofreading.

Use the word **error** when the student consistently produces spoken or written forms that differ from the standard and these nonstandard forms are likely the result of the student not knowing the rule or standard, or applying a false rule or standard. For example, the misspellings:

*fone        oxes        elefant        childs*

are errors. They show the student does not yet know the "ph" spelling of "f" and plural forms of common irregular nouns. The correction of an error is a matter for instruction.

| Common Errors | Examples |
|---|---|
| Adds articles | After *the* work, Jorge went home.<br>We got *a* good news about our jobs.<br>We need eggs and *a* sugar. |
| Adds -s | Ana must write*s* a letter.<br>Does he watch*es* TV everyday? |
| Adds -ing | He does work*ing* on the car.<br>He should mow*ing* the lawn. |
| Adds (to) do | *Does* he can fix the wheel?<br>He *does* can fix the wheel. |
| Omits articles | I gave *(the)* box to *(the)* nurse.<br>She is *(the)* aunt of *(the)* girl.<br>He was *(a)* brave soldier. |
| Substitutes article | We have *a* prettiest house in the neighborhood.<br>Do you have *the* question? |
| Tense shift | Tomorrow we *will go* to the shopping center and *have to buy sneakers for gym class.* |
| Not parallel | William was a good *president* and *smart.*<br>*Picking* the berries, *making* the jam and *the savings* are fun. |
| Not in agreement | The *flowers grows* in the garden.<br>The *doctor and nurse speaks* to the patient.<br>*Everybody have* a name. |

The baseball *player and the coach has* taken *his* place*(s)* on the stage.

Person shift
*Becky and Zim* took the bus to the pier on the island and then *we* walked to the cottage.

Incomplete sentence
Children *(are)* playing in the park.
Commuters *(were)* running to catch their trains.

Wrong order
I gave *to him* the tickets.
*On the shelf* the book was found.

Wrong pronoun
Jesse and *me* did the homework.
Jesse and I did *their* homework.
The pilots check *his* baggage.

Wrong word
There are *less* people in the audience today than yesterday.
The little girl is very *handsome*.
He was not *conscience* when he arrived at the hospital.

# 4–9 HELPING STUDENTS WITH AUDIENCE RECOGNITION

Communication takes two—a speaker and a listener, or a writer and a reader. Effective communication, either spoken or written, means the audience—the listeners or readers—understands the message. To help listeners and readers get the message, change the way you speak and write to match the audience and the circumstances. These adaptations are sometimes called **registers**. Before speaking or writing, consider

- the age of the audience;
- your social relationship;
- their knowledge of the subject;
- the subject itself;
- the purpose of the communication.

*Age of audience*—Children's knowledge of language and of the world is limited, and their ability to deal with complicated information is not well developed. When speaking or writing to children, use a narrative style with common words and basic sentence structures. Keep the message simple and brief.

An older, more mature audience has a full command of language and a broader understanding of the world. Adults can understand complex information if it is clearly presented. When communicating with adults, use explicit vocabulary. Vary sentence structure, including both simple and complex sentences. The message may draw upon commonly known or experienced phenomena; it may be detailed. Lengthy messages must be organized in order to be easily understood.

*Social relationship*—There are many types of social relationships including those between parents and children, among family members, between teachers and students, between employers and employees, between individuals and those in authority, between individuals and those in religious or other respected positions, among friends, between spouses, between strangers, and between older and younger persons.

The relationship between the speaker and listener, or writer and reader, affects several aspects of the communication. It will determine the level of respect that needs to be conveyed and the degree of familiarity and shared experiences that can be relied upon.

These factors determine the greeting, tone, structure, vocabulary, level of detail or completeness, appropriateness of slang or jargon, and suitability of personal referents.

*Knowledge of subject*—Estimate how much the audience knows about the subject by considering their age and education, their employment, and their social status. Sometimes personal background, such as where one grew up or one's ethnicity, will help to estimate their level of knowledge of a subject.

The audience's knowledge of the subject will determine the level of detail and explanation that is necessary, as well as the type of vocabulary that is suitable.

124

*Subject matter*—Subject matter covers a range from common to uncommon; from serious to humorous; from technical to general; from scientific to affective; and so on. Subject factors will help to determine what vocabulary, tone, and level of detail to use.

*Purpose of communication*—Communication has a purpose: to tell a story, to ask a question, to give directions, to share a joke, to make a request, to exhort, to show affection, and so forth. The purpose affects the tone, vocabulary, and structures.

## AUDIENCE ERRORS

The audience errors of nonnative speakers of English are often the result of cultural transfer or language instruction. When students transfer the rules for registers from their native languages and cultures to American English, the results may be inappropriate. For example, what might be perfectly acceptable for a target audience in Spain may be too formal, too flowery, and too indirect in the United States.

Language instruction also plays a part in some students' audience errors. For some, ESL instruction focuses heavily on conversational elements. This leaves the students without knowledge of the more formal and/or academic vocabulary and grammar structures. For others, language instruction is focused on "book" work— grammar, academic vocabulary, and reading, leaving students with little knowledge of colloquial expressions, idiomatic usage, and informal grammatical constructions.

Some activities that help students develop a proper audience sense include role playing, rewriting dialogue or other material to suit different audiences, and comparing written and spoken samples addressed to different groups.

# SECTION 5
# Pronunciation

# 5-1 CONSONANT CHART

|  | Flow of Air | | Use of Vocal Chords | | Articulation | | | Air Passage | |
|---|---|---|---|---|---|---|---|---|---|
|  | Stop | Continuant | Voiced | Unvoiced | Dental | Lingual | Labial | Nasal | Oral |
| b | x |  | x |  |  |  | x |  | x |
| d | x |  | x |  |  | x |  |  | x |
| f |  | x |  | x | x |  | x |  | x |
| g | x |  | x |  |  | x |  |  | x |
| h |  | x |  | x |  |  |  |  | x |
| k | x |  |  | x |  | x |  |  | x |
| l |  | x | x |  |  | x |  |  | x |
| m |  | x | x |  |  |  | x | x |  |
| n |  | x | x |  |  | x |  | x |  |
| ng |  | x | x |  |  | x |  | x |  |
| p | x |  |  | x |  |  | x |  | x |
| r |  | x | x |  |  |  | x |  | x |
| s |  | x |  | x |  | x |  |  | x |
| sh |  | x |  | x |  |  | x |  | x |
| t | x |  | x |  |  | x |  |  | x |
| th |  | x |  | x | x | x |  |  | x |
| *th* |  | x | x |  | x | x |  |  | x |
| v |  | x | x |  | x | x |  |  | x |
| w |  | x | x |  |  |  | x |  | x |
| y |  | x | x |  |  | x |  |  | x |
| ż |  | x | x |  |  | x |  |  | x |
| s |  | x | x |  |  |  | x |  | x |
| ch | x |  |  | x |  |  | x |  | x |
| dg | x |  | x |  |  |  | x |  | x |

# 5–2  *VOWEL CHART*

| Vowel sound | Key word | Tongue position | Lip position | Facial muscles |
|---|---|---|---|---|
| ē | me | high - front | unrounded | tensed |
| i | hit | high - front | unrounded | relaxed |
| ā | ate | mid to high - front | unrounded | tensed |
| e | let | mid - front | unrounded | relaxed |
| a | sat | low - front | unrounded | relaxed |
| o | hot | low - center | unrounded | relaxed |
| u | hut | mid - center | unrounded | relaxed |
| aw | saw | low - back | slightly rounded | tensed |
| ō | so | mid to high - back | round-more round | tensed |
| oo | look | high - back | rounded | relaxed |
| o͞o | cool | high - back | very rounded | tensed |
| ī | kite | low/high - center/front | unrounded | tensed |
| ow | cow | low/high - center/back | unrounded-round | tensed |
| oy | boy | low/high - back/front | round-unrounded | tensed |

VOWEL PROGRESSION:

Pete, pit, pate, pet, pat, pot, putt, Paul, pole, pull, pool

# 5–3 PROBLEM ENGLISH SOUNDS FOR SPEAKERS OF OTHER LANGUAGES

| Native language | Problem English sounds |
|---|---|
| **Chinese** | b ch d dg f g̑ j l m n ng ō sh s th *th* v z l-clusters r-clusters |
| **French** | ā ch ē h j ng oo oy s th *th* s shwa |
| **Greek** | aw b d ē g i j m n ng oo r s w y z shwa end clusters |
| **Italian** | a ar dg h i ng th *th* v shwa l-clusters end clusters |
| **Japanese** | dg f h i l th *th* oo r sh s v w shwa l-clusters r-clusters |
| **Korean** | b l ō ow p r sh t *th* l-clusters r-clusters |
| **Spanish** | b d dg h j m n ng r sh t th v w y z s-clusters end clusters |
| **Urdu** | ā a d ē e f n ng s sh t th *th* |
| **Vietnamese** | ā ē k l ng p r sh s y l-clusters r-clusters |

# 5-4 PROBLEM ENGLISH CONTRASTS FOR SPEAKERS OF OTHER LANGUAGES

| Problem Contrast | Chinese | French | Greek | Italian | Japanese | Korean | Spanish | Urdu | Vietnamese |
|---|---|---|---|---|---|---|---|---|---|
| ā/a | | | x | x | x | x | | x | |
| ā/e | | | x | x | x | x | x | x | x |
| a/e | x | | x | x | x | x | x | x | x |
| a/o | x | x | x | x | x | x | x | x | x |
| a/u | x | | x | x | x | | x | x | |
| ē/i | x | x | x | x | x | x | x | x | x |
| e/u | x | | x | x | | | x | x | |
| ō/o | x | | x | x | x | | x | x | x |
| o/aw | x | | x | | x | x | x | x | x |
| o/u | x | | x | x | x | | x | | x |
| u/o͞o | x | x | x | x | | | x | x | x |
| u/oo | x | | x | | | x | | x | x |
| u/aw | x | | x | x | x | x | x | x | |
| o͞o/oo | x | x | | x | | x | x | x | |
| b/p | x | | | | | x | x | | x |
| b/v | | | x | | x | x | x | | |
| ch/j | | | | x | | x | x | | x |
| ch/sh | x | x | x | | x | x | x | | x |
| d/*th* | x | | | x | x | x | x | x | x |
| f/th | | | | x | | x | x | x | x |
| l/r | x | | | | x | x | x | | x |
| n/ng | x | x | x | x | x | | x | x | |
| s/sh | | | x | x | x | x | x | | x |
| s/th | x | x | | x | x | x | x | x | x |
| s/z | x | | x | x | | x | x | | x |
| sh/th | | | | x | x | x | x | x | x |
| t/th | x | | | x | x | x | x | x | x |
| th/*th* | x | x | | x | x | x | x | x | x |
| *th*/z | x | x | x | x | x | x | x | x | x |

# 5-5 ENGLISH SOUNDS NOT IN OTHER LANGUAGES

There are sounds regularly used in English that are not part of other languages. In general, the sounds listed below are not part of the other languages' regular sound systems, although they may occur in certain dialects, or in restricted use, such as in the medial position in a word. These sounds are difficult for new speakers of English for two reasons: first, students have not had any practice recognizing these sounds or discriminating them from others; and, second, because students have not used these sounds before, they have had no practice pronouncing them.

To master these sounds, students will need to learn to recognize them through auditory discrimination training, then learn to produce them through practice with minimal pairs and repetition of the phonemes in the initial, medial, and final positions in words.

| Language | Sounds Not Part of the Language |
|---|---|
| Chinese | b  ch  d  dg  g  oa  sh  *s*  th  *th*  v  z |
| French | ch  ee  j  ng  oo  th  *th* |
| Greek | aw  ee  i  oo  schwa |
| Italian | a  ar  dg  h  i  ng  th  *th*  schwa |
| Japanese | dg  f  i  th  *th*  oo  v  schwa |
| Spanish | dg  j  sh  th  z |

# 5–6 PRACTICE FOR PROBLEM CONTRASTS AND SOUNDS

**ā/a**

| | | |
|---|---|---|
| bake back | fade fad | cape cap |
| base bass | rain ran | haze has |
| played plaid | rake rack | shame sham |
| brain bran | mate mat | slate slat |
| gale gal | lace lass | aid add |

**ā/e**

| | | |
|---|---|---|
| bait bet | late let | gate get |
| aid Ed | raid red | rake wreck |
| paper pepper | fade fed | wait wet |
| Yale yell | sale sell | lace less |
| taste test | wade wed | waist west |

**a/e**

| | | |
|---|---|---|
| pack peck | mass mess | dad dead |
| sat set | lad led | vary very |
| mat met | land lend | bag beg |
| dance dense | pat pet | land lend |
| pan pen | laughed left | past pest |

**a/ī**

| | | |
|---|---|---|
| cat kite | mat might | fat fight |
| dam dime | fan fine | Dan dine |
| bran brine | dad died | flat flight |
| clam climb | back bike | grand grind |
| lack like | mack Mike | man mine |

**a/i**

| | | |
|---|---|---|
| pan pin | ban bin | knack nick |
| sat sit | fat fit | cat kit |
| stack stick | pack pick | cast kissed |
| draft drift | wax wicks | track trick |
| slam slim | drank drink | dad did |

**a/o**

| | | |
|---|---|---|
| hat hot | pat pot | cat cot |
| hag hog | mass moss | lack lock |
| rat rot | bag bog | flack flock |
| rack rock | cad cod | ax ox |
| black block | racket rocket | chap chop |

**a/u**

| | | |
|---|---|---|
| rag rug | calf cuff | ankle uncle |
| back buck | branch brunch | gal gull |
| lag lug | track truck | slam slum |
| patter putter | dance dunce | rang rung |
| badge budge | rash rush | bank bunk |

**ē/i**

| | | |
|---|---|---|
| Pete pit | meat mitt | read rid |
| feet fit | deep dip | seen sin |

134

|        |              |              |              |
|--------|--------------|--------------|--------------|
|        | sleep slip   | seek sick    | seat sit     |
|        | week wick    | teen tin     | wheeze whiz  |
|        | sleek slick  | bean bin     | fleet flit   |
| e/i    | let lit      | pet pit      | set sit      |
|        | check chick  | ten tin      | spell spill  |
|        | hell hill    | peg pig      | etch itch    |
|        | weather wither | left lift  | mess miss    |
|        | better bitter | bell bill   | lest list    |
| e/o    | pep pop      | den Don      | get got      |
|        | check chock  | net not      | deck dock    |
|        | said sod     | penned pond  | pet pot      |
|        | yet yacht    | debt dot     | fleck flock  |
|        | leg log      | keg cog      | bend bond    |
| e/u    | bed bud      | pep pup      | best bust    |
|        | meddle muddle | pen pun     | pedal puddle |
|        | desk dusk    | dell dull    | flesh flush  |
|        | dead dud     | dense dunce  | bench bunch  |
|        | check chuck  | deck duck    | bet but      |
| i/o    | pit pot      | tip top      | clip clop    |
|        | nib knob     | kid cod      | Sid sod      |
|        | flick flock  | tick tock    | lick lock    |
|        | click clock  | Nick knock   | picket pocket |
|        | rickets rockets | spit spot | slit slot    |
| i/u    | pin pun      | bin bun      | rim rum      |
|        | sin sun      | din done     | biddy buddy  |
|        | bid bud      | tin ton      | fin fun      |
|        | lick luck    | trick truck  | stick stuck  |
|        | miss muss    | tress truss  | mitt mutt    |
| ō/o    | road rod     | hope hop     | goat got     |
|        | folks fox    | holy holly   | note not     |
|        | slope slop   | smoke smock  | soak sock    |
|        | robe rob     | cloak clock  | cone con     |
|        | coat cot     | mope mop     | tote tot     |
| o/aw   | odd awed     | Don dawn     | not naught   |
|        | tot taught   | cot caught   | sod sawed    |
|        | hock hawk    | stock stalk  | knotty naughty |
|        | fond fawned  | clod clawed  | collar caller |
|        | body bawdy   | pod pawed    | pond pawned  |
| o/u    | pot put      | lost lust    | lock luck    |
|        | boss bus     | model muddle | rot rut      |

|  | | | |
|---|---|---|---|
| | dog dug | hot hut | gosh gush |
| | pop pup | shot shut | robbed rubbed |
| | cot cut | dock duck | smog smug |
| **u/o͞o** | pull pool | full fool | soot suit |
| | look Luke | hood who'd | could cooed |
| | but boot | stood stewed | should shoed |
| **u/oo** | tuck took | luck look | buck book |
| | stud stood | putt put | Huck's hooks |
| | cud could | huff hoff | shuck shook |
| **u/aw** | cull call | gull gall | fun fawn |
| | cruller crawler | bus boss | flood flawed |
| | bud baud | thud thawed | bubble bauble |
| | hunch haunch | lunch launch | punch paunch |
| **o͞o/oo** | wooed would | cooed could | shoed should |
| | pool pull | stewed stood | Luke look |
| **b/p** | bade paid | bin pin | big pig |
| | cub cup | back pack | bet pet |
| | by pie | beat Pete | mob mop |
| | bale pale | boast post | bony pony |
| | beach peach | batter patter | bee pea |
| **b/v** | boat vote | bet vet | robe rove |
| | berry very | bend vend | cabs calves |
| | bat vat | ban van | best vest |
| | bolt volt | curb curve | bane vane |
| | saber savor | bicker vicker | lobes loaves |
| **ch/j** | chin gin | chain Jane | chest jest |
| | choke joke | cheap jeep | etch edge |
| | chill Jill | cheer jerr | chip gyp |
| | char jar | chunk junk | searches surges |
| | cinch singe | choice Joyce | chug jug |
| **ch/sh** | chew shoe | chop shop | chip ship |
| | witch wish | cheap sheep | match mash |
| | choose shoes | much mush | chair share |
| | chore shore | cheer sheer | chin shin |
| | cherry sherry | chew shoe | watch wash |
| **d/*th*** | den then | dine thine | day they |
| | dough though | dare their | ladder lather |
| | bade bathe | seed seethe | breed breathe |
| | Dan than | dense thence | die thy |
| | loads loathes | wordy worthy | ride writhe |

*The ESL Teacher's Book of Lists*, © 1993 by John Wiley & Sons, Inc.

| f/th | | | |
|---|---|---|---|
| | fin thin | free three | frill thrill |
| | fret threat | fought thought | fresh thresh |
| | Fred thread | first thirst | miff myth |
| | oaf oath | reef wreath | roof Ruth |
| | deaf death | half hath | laughs laths |

| l/r | | | |
|---|---|---|---|
| | loyal royal | lay ray | law raw |
| | led red | low row | lax racks |
| | list wrist | lake rake | sill sir |
| | lap wrap | goal gore | load road |
| | late rate | lung rung | tile tire |

| s/sh | | | |
|---|---|---|---|
| | same shame | sack shack | seat sheet |
| | sign shine | self shelf | sealed shield |
| | sock shock | sift shift | sake shake |
| | save shave | seer sheer | sore shore |
| | sigh shy | sell shell | sail shale |

| s/th | | | |
|---|---|---|---|
| | sigh thigh | sick thick | seem theme |
| | sank thank | saw thaw | sin thin |
| | sink think | sought thought | some thumb |
| | sump thump | face faith | pass path |
| | mass math | mouse mouth | moss moth |

| s/z | | | |
|---|---|---|---|
| | bus buzz | sip zip | peace peas |
| | hiss his | close clothes | face phase |
| | sue zoo | dice dies | sink zinc |
| | seal zeal | sewn zone | price prize |
| | since sins | fuss fuzz | rice rise |

| sh/th | | | |
|---|---|---|---|
| | shy thigh | shred thread | shrill thrill |
| | shin thin | sheaf thief | shank thank |
| | shrew through | frosh froth | harsh hearth |
| | lash lath | mash math | rash rath |

| t/th | | | |
|---|---|---|---|
| | tin thin | tick thick | taught thought |
| | true threw | tinker thinker | teem theme |
| | tank thank | tie thigh | ticket thicket |
| | tong thong | taught thought | trash thrash |
| | tug thug | tree three | true threw |

| th/*th* | | | |
|---|---|---|---|
| | thigh thy | teeth teethe | lath lathe |
| | sooth soothe | ether either | bath bathe |

| *th*/z | | | |
|---|---|---|---|
| | lather lazer | seethe seize | thee Z |
| | teethe tease | then Zen | breathe breeze |

## L-CLUSTERS

| bl | cl | fl | gl | pl | sl | spl |
|----|----|----|----|----|----|-----|
| blast | class | flask | glass | place | slice | splash |
| blue | clue | flew | glue | plum | slave | splat |
| blood | claim | flame | gleem | please | sleeve | splice |
| black | clear | fled | glum | plight | slight | spleen |
| bliss | clinic | flicker | glade | plain | slow | splint |
| blouse | cloth | float | glow | plow | slim | splendor |
| blind | climate | flight | glider | plant | slam | split |
| blur | cloak | flood | glove | pledge | sled | splurge |
| bleed | clef | flock | glitter | plant | slew | splendid |
| blade | club | flea | gloom | plod | slope | splinter |

## R-CLUSTERS

| br | cr | dr | fr | gr | pr |
|----|----|----|----|----|----|
| brat | cram | drive | free | great | prize |
| brick | crock | dream | frost | green | praise |
| broom | creek | drain | friend | grass | practice |
| brave | crib | drew | frame | grow | pretty |
| break | cross | drape | from | groom | prune |
| breed | creed | dread | freak | Greek | princess |
| brother | crane | drip | fruit | gray | pray |
| brisk | crumb | drove | frozen | grown | produce |
| bright | cry | drum | fright | grime | prime |
| broad | crude | dragon | fret | gradual | prepare |

| tr | scr | spr | str | thr |
|----|----|----|----|----|
| train | scream | spring | street | through |
| trade | screech | sprig | stream | throat |
| trim | scrimp | sprung | string | thrive |
| threat | scrape | sprang | struggle | throne |
| treadle | scram | spree | straight | thread |
| trust | scrounge | sprinkle | strive | three |
| try | scroll | sprawl | strum | thrash |
| trial | scratch | sprite | stretch | throw |
| true | screw | spray | strain | thrift |
| trap | script | sprout | straw | thrill |

## S-CLUSTERS

| sc/sk | scr | sl | sm | sn |
|-------|-----|----|----|----|
| scar | screen | slip | small | sneeze |
| scare | scratch | slap | smell | snack |

*The ESL Teacher's Book of Lists,* © 1993 by John Wiley & Sons, Inc.

| sc/sk | scr | sl | sm | sn *(continued)* |
|-------|-----|-----|-----|-----|
| score | scrub | slept | smack | snow |
| scorn | scrape | slum | smear | snip |
| scout | screw | slump | smile | snob |
| skid | scram | sleep | smooth | sniff |
| skate | scrap | slay | smother | snake |
| skill | scrambled | slick | smoke | snap |
| ski | screech | slouch | smash | sneak |
| skunk | scribble | slim | smirk | snoop |

| sh | sp/spr | st/str | sw | squ |
|-----|--------|--------|-----|-----|
| shell | spite | stick | sweet | squeeze |
| ship | space | stuck | swim | squid |
| shape | spice | stone | sweat | squeak |
| shimmer | speak | steak | swagger | squash |
| shout | spend | stare | sway | square |
| sheep | spring | street | swipe | squint |
| shine | sprint | stream | sworn | squire |
| shadow | spry | stray | swear | squad |
| shoot | spray | stride | swat | squaw |
| show | sprain | strove | swell | squeal |

## END CLUSTERS

| mp | nd | ng | nk | nt | st | nch |
|-----|-----|-----|-----|-----|-----|-----|
| lamp | land | sang | sank | saint | list | inch |
| damp | sand | sung | bank | pint | mist | hunch |
| champ | brand | hang | blank | pant | lost | lunch |
| tramp | grand | bang | thank | ant | mast | pinch |
| stamp | send | sing | crank | bent | crust | cinch |
| clamp | blend | sting | dank | sent | least | bunch |
| dump | tend | among | trunk | splint | host | crunch |
| jump | round | song | pink | lint | ghost | ranch |
| bump | kind | bring | think | flint | just | branch |
| crimp | mind | hung | bunk | hunt | must | staunch |

# 5-7 PRACTICE FOR PHONEMES IN THE INITIAL POSITION

**CONSONANTS**

| English Spellings | Practice Words | | | | |
|---|---|---|---|---|---|
| b | bat | bay | boy | bit | bug |
| | bee | bun | belt | bike | box |
| | bake | bail | boar | bath | bow |
| | boat | bone | bar | beat | bough |
| c, k | can | cane | corn | cub | cone |
| | connect | cube | code | cot | call |
| | country | come | car | cash | cool |
| | cater | coast | cause | curl | cat |
| | kit | kite | key | kind | kiss |
| | kick | keep | kettle | kale | keel |
| | kennel | kidney | kilt | king | kink |
| | kin | kill | kindle | kitchen | kitty |
| ch | check | chair | chin | cheat | chum |
| | chess | chap | chime | choose | chill |
| | child | choice | chomp | chick | chat |
| | chuck | chain | char | chose | charm |
| d | dad | dare | door | daze | day |
| | deep | dell | do | dough | die |
| | dirt | dim | doll | deer | dune |
| | dot | dust | dean | dump | dash |
| f | fat | for | fir | fine | fast |
| | feet | find | fun | food | foot |
| | fed | fate | fall | fence | faint |
| | feather | foil | fear | fire | foe |
| g | got | get | gold | good | game |
| | girl | gun | gather | geese | goal |
| | gauge | gall | gore | gutter | gash |
| | gain | gape | gone | gave | gift |
| h | hat | head | heed | hug | his |
| | hate | herd | hurt | have | hope |
| | hive | hilt | hero | hag | harm |
| | hire | high | howl | horse | hoe |
| j, g | jam | jet | joy | jetty | joke |
| | jaw | January | juice | jute | jaunt |
| | jeans | jolly | jeep | jail | jig |
| | jack | junk | jelly | Jew | jury |

140

The ESL Teacher's Book of Lists, © 1993 by John Wiley & Sons, Inc.

| English Spellings | Practice Words | | | | |
|---|---|---|---|---|---|
| j, g | gem | gym | gentle | ginger | germ |
| | gypsy | gin | gene | giant | geode |
| | general | gender | generous | gerbil | gent |
| | gist | giraffe | gyrate | genius | gyp |
| l | lit | late | lost | load | light |
| | low | loose | lime | library | let |
| | lease | lead | lack | limb | law |
| | lay | loom | lush | lug | lock |
| m | mat | meet | made | music | metal |
| | more | mitten | much | might | most |
| | moth | mink | mine | mix | mute |
| | mood | mourn | mere | malt | myth |
| n, gn, kn | net | nice | nature | north | not |
| | neat | neither | now | new | nag |
| | numb | notice | nick | never | naked |
| | near | noose | nine | node | nurse |
| | gnash | gnarl | gnome | gnaw | gnat |
| | knit | knee | knot | knock | known |
| | kneel | knight | knack | knob | knave |
| | knead | know | knoll | knuckle | knew |
| | knowledge | knife | knapsack | knickers | knell |
| p | path | pain | peat | pen | pit |
| | pine | pose | point | power | Paul |
| | paw | pallor | purse | port | poem |
| | pot | paste | pass | perk | pun |
| qu | quick | queen | quasar | quest | queer |
| | quack | quaint | quite | qualify | quote |
| | quadrant | quantum | queasy | quart | quiz |
| | quilt | question | quiet | quality | quit |
| r, wr | rest | rose | rain | rattle | rib |
| | ride | rein | reach | report | ruin |
| | run | room | rob | rabbit | rape |
| | right | route | row | raw | roar |
| | write | wring | wrestle | wren | wreck |
| | wrap | wrath | wreath | wrench | wry |
| | wrong | writer | wriggle | wretch | wrist |
| s, c | set | soft | south | sane | seek |
| | seat | sow | sand | sable | said |
| | say | sign | sight | sick | saw |
| | symbol | sore | suds | sure | sue |
| | city | circle | celery | celebrate | cell |
| | cement | century | cemetery | center | cent |

| English Spellings | Practice Words | | | | |
|---|---|---|---|---|---|
| s, c | cyclone | certain | citrus | cirrus | civil |
| | cite | circulate | circuit | circus | cycle |
| sh | show | share | sheet | shame | ship |
| | shop | shape | Shetland | shine | shear |
| | shed | sheep | shepherd | shy | shell |
| | shoal | shin | shackle | shrimp | shark |
| t | teeth | tone | tether | tons | table |
| | tan | tame | tune | tunnel | tax |
| | tooth | touch | tow | two | tide |
| | toe | tire | tied | talk | took |
| th | think | thistle | thief | thieves | thin |
| | thatch | thank | thaw | theater | theme |
| | theory | theology | theorem | thermal | thick |
| | thesis | thimble | thigh | thicket | thorn |
| *th* | these | they | those | this | then |
| | the | than | their | thence | that |
| | there | thine | thou | thy | thus |
| v | vain | vegetable | violet | visor | vet |
| | verb | veer | view | vex | verse |
| | vote | voice | vow | vat | vigor |
| | volt | vying | vein | vent | vapor |
| w | wish | want | wane | wax | wet |
| | we | wire | wore | won | would |
| | wood | worry | war | wall | woe |
| | win | woman | wail | wine | worse |
| y | yet | yam | yeast | yore | Yale |
| | yak | yard | yawn | yellow | yea |
| | you | yolk | yacht | yowl | yell |
| | year | young | youth | yodel | yen |
| z | zoo | zero | zip | zest | zebra |
| | zipper | zenith | zinc | zoom | zany |
| | zeal | zing | zone | zodiac | zip |
| | Zen | zephyr | zither | zinnia | Zeus |

## Vowels

| English Spellings | Practice Words | | | | |
|---|---|---|---|---|---|
| a, ai, a_e | able | aim | ate | acre | Asia |
| | age | ache | ailment | aid | ace |
| | acorn | acreage | aorta | agency | ain't |
| | angel | ancient | amen | Amish | ale |

*The ESL Teacher's Book of Lists*, © 1993 by John Wiley & Sons, Inc.

| English Spellings | Practice Words | | | | |
|---|---|---|---|---|---|
| a | apple | accident | advice | alcove | add |
| | actress | acrobat | animal | attic | as |
| | activity | adhere | afghan | aggravate | after |
| | album | alto | amble | anarchy | apt |
| au, aw, al | auto | awful | autumn | automatic | awe |
| | always | awning | awkward | author | all |
| | audience | audit | audible | authentic | also |
| | almost | almanac | audition | augment | alter |
| e, ee, ea | equal | ego | easy | eel | each |
| | even | evil | east | eagle | ear |
| | easel | evenly | edict | equinox | eaten |
| | either | eerie | ether | evening | ethos |
| e | exit | edit | epic | empty | elk |
| | elbow | edge | elder | emphasis | else |
| | enemy | educate | embalm | empathy | ebb |
| | endive | essay | ethnic | every | etch |
| i, i_e | ice | icy | icing | idle | ideal |
| | identity | idea | island | iodine | idol |
| | ion | irate | iris | iron | ivory |
| | ivy | item | isotope | isle | ire |
| i | ignite | itch | idiom | ignore | ill |
| | image | imagine | impact | improve | ink |
| | inch | indeed | Indian | index | inept |
| | induct | invest | install | insure | if |
| o, oa, o_e, ow | oasis | oats | opus | over | obey |
| | open | own | ocean | oboe | okra |
| | odor | omit | owe | oak | oath |
| | owner | old | opium | ode | opal |
| o | otter | opera | option | observe | odd |
| | opt | optical | opposite | oxygen | oxide |
| | Oscar | osprey | osmosis | opulent | oxen |
| | operate | ominous | octopus | onto | olive |
| or | orchid | orchestra | orate | orator | orb |
| | order | orange | ordeal | orderly | orbit |
| | ornate | oregano | organ | organize | ore |
| u, u_e | unit | uniform | union | united | usual |
| | universe | utilize | unique | unicorn | unity |
| | unanimous | unify | unison | universal | uses |
| | uranium | Uranus | Utopia | utility | use |

| English Spellings | Practice Words | | | | |
|---|---|---|---|---|---|
| u | ugly | ulna | ugh | udder | uncle |
| | ulcer | ultra | umbrella | umpire | under |
| | upper | uphold | upward | upset | upon |
| | utter | usher | uprise | ultimate | until |
| schwa a, o, u | about | affront | afford | amend | adapt |
| | abuse | amuse | among | apart | apply |
| | appear | assist | astound | address | aside |
| | assault | attest | astute | avoid | away |
| | object | opossum | oblige | observe | occur |
| | occult | oppress | oppose | obsession | obtain |
| | umbrella | unarmed | upon | unwise | untie |

*The ESL Teacher's Book of Lists,* © 1993 by John Wiley & Sons, Inc.

# 5-8 PRACTICE FOR PHONEMES IN THE MEDIAL POSITION

## CONSONANTS

| English Spellings | Practice Words | | | | |
|---|---|---|---|---|---|
| b | pebble | number | rubber | object | Bobby |
| | bribe | problem | probably | rabbit | robber |
| | babble | bible | embryo | terrible | ruby |
| | robbery | acrobat | hobbled | treble | table |
| c, k | picture | pucker | decree | backer | uncap |
| | preclude | because | second | attacker | acorn |
| | package | sticky | spackle | speckle | picky |
| | pocket | picket | parking | tractor | liked |
| ch | purchase | merchant | preacher | teacher | achoo |
| | hunches | trenches | benches | beaches | inches |
| | bleacher | exchange | recharge | unchain | itchy |
| d | daddy | bleeding | siding | ladder | tidal |
| | trader | bidder | garden | pudding | codes |
| | fading | buddy | under | undress | hides |
| | muddy | wedding | cuddle | seedling | raids |
| f | offer | after | effort | effect | oft |
| | infidel | infest | afford | differ | rifle |
| | refuse | safety | sniffle | refine | unfed |
| | crafty | leftist | sifter | shifty | lofty |
| g | giggle | logger | regress | English | anger |
| | region | danger | origin | ogre | rigor |
| | juggle | baggage | digger | rigging | wagon |
| | piggy | stagger | argon | organ | muggy |
| h | behave | inhale | unhinge | unhappy | ahead |
| | adhere | rehire | behold | inhabit | ahoy |
| | inherent | rehash | behalf | behead | unhook |
| | beholden | behind | unhealthy | perhaps | unholy |
| j, g, dg | wager | aging | ranger | merger | ajar |
| | adjourn | adjacent | adjust | adjunct | agent |
| | larger | margin | badger | fragile | angel |
| | agile | agitate | agenda | paging | fudgy |
| l | million | fellow | follow | mallard | silly |
| | gallon | felon | melody | stellar | melon |
| | feeling | teller | bailer | ballot | oily |
| | ballast | bowler | crawling | wallet | jelly |

| English Spellings | Practice Words | | | | |
|---|---|---|---|---|---|
| m | hammer | steamer | amend | stammer | homey |
| | steamy | clammy | number | example | mommy |
| | chemical | tremor | calmer | stampede | army |
| | cramming | trample | sample | stamina | armor |
| n, gn, kn | minute | winning | chinning | ground | any |
| | frown | sinner | banner | thinner | tiny |
| | handy | window | winter | banana | tenor |
| | dinner | slander | calendar | lender | dense |
| ng | singing | wings | bands | clanged | fangs |
| | single | finger | winged | mingle | tongs |
| | bringing | langor | languish | tingle | pings |
| | springy | spangled | language | linguist | anger |
| p | paper | dapper | zipper | competent | opera |
| | depend | caption | happy | impress | apple |
| | preppy | upper | helpless | puppy | super |
| | pepper | copper | sweeper | important | caper |
| qu | acquaint | acquire | acquit | inquire | |
| | require | request | aqua | inquiry | |
| r | mirror | earring | warrior | warts | party |
| | jarring | berry | furry | prying | fury |
| | correct | error | sherry | sorry | worry |
| | curry | bury | carry | boring | barn |
| s, c | assent | acid | fussy | sissy | also |
| | assist | aside | mossy | sister | list |
| | mister | slicer | absent | abscissa | nicer |
| | racer | accent | twisted | brisk | ask |
| sh | lashes | worship | kinship | crashed | wishes |
| | bushy | crushed | finishing | fresher | mashed |
| | freshman | fashion | marshes | cashes | mushy |
| | ashore | seashore | wishing | leashed | washer |
| *s* | measure | treasure | pleasure | vision | fissure |
| t | chatter | matter | pattern | little | actor |
| | faster | mortar | mitten | tomato | motor |
| | sitting | gifted | mountain | attend | meter |
| | catalog | notebook | cottage | lettuce | altar |
| th | author | authentic | athlete | rethink | ether |
| | nothing | python | faithful | bathroom | Cathy |
| | moths | something | Ethan | anthem | ethic |
| *th* | either | bathers | lather | father | mother |
| | clothing | brother | weather | other | bother |

*The ESL Teacher's Book of Lists*, © 1993 by John Wiley & Sons, Inc.

| English Spellings | Practice Words | | | | |
|---|---|---|---|---|---|
| v | invade | invoice | evolution | evolve | evade |
|   | evening | event | eventual | evergreen | even |
|   | every | every | Everest | avarice | aver |
|   | adverse | adversary | invert | covert | cover |
| w | reward | rewind | forward | awaken | |
|   | inward | halfway | sidewalk | midway | |
|   | Darwin | dogwood | Edward | coward | |
|   | bewilder | beeswax | aware | away | |
| y | lawyer | beyond | canyon | vineyard | |
|   | mayor | sawyer | payee | backyard | |
| z, s | lazy | busy | puzzle | pretzel | |
|   | embezzle | jazzy | quizzical | fizzy | |
|   | wizard | fuzzy | wisdom | wizen | |
|   | buzzard | citizen | scissors | dozen | |

## VOWELS

| English Spellings | Practice Words | | | | |
|---|---|---|---|---|---|
| a, ai, a_e | table | rain | fame | bathe | gable |
|   | baby | save | place | trade | grave |
|   | dame | face | slain | matron | lake |
|   | grain | brace | shade | slate | fade |
| a | crab | glad | grand | scrap | flat |
|   | span | bran | rack | stack | drab |
|   | captive | tractor | cabin | flag | pass |
|   | Patty | jacket | spackle | class | snag |
| au, aw, al | drawn | lawn | pawn | stalled | salt |
|   | brawn | yawn | clawed | called | malt |
|   | halted | fault | vault | cauldron | Walt |
| e, ee, ea | behold | beef | veer | meat | keep |
|   | teach | wheat | squeal | speak | rerun |
|   | redeem | greeting | steeple | really | deal |
|   | sweet | streak | speed | spear | leaky |
| e | best | spend | smell | letter | send |
|   | better | lesson | pedal | federal | shred |
|   | vest | sled | text | quest | then |
|   | strength | stench | crest | fender | fret |
| i, i_e, igh | tripod | bicycle | dime | shrine | wide |
|   | spicy | rice | crime | diner | tiny |
|   | mind | prime | bright | might | fighter |
|   | sight | size | drive | quite | five |

| English Spellings | Practice Words | | | | |
|---|---|---|---|---|---|
| i | sit | trip | grip | knit | skit |
| | skid | sick | skinny | bitter | kick |
| | timid | victim | vigor | wicker | gin |
| | mitten | mist | middle | mixture | kiss |
| o, oa, o_e | gold | zone | phone | boat | moldy |
| | goat | clone | joke | coke | cone |
| | stolen | bolt | broke | coat | bone |
| | gross | toast | bloat | hope | home |
| o | crop | frog | bottle | copper | body |
| | rocky | Bobby | robber | jogger | jock |
| | jolly | shot | drop | blotter | shop |
| | box | stock | snob | block | copy |
| oi, oy | royal | boil | soil | cloister | toil |
| oo | book | foot | brook | took | good |
| | hood | crook | wool | goodbye | hoof |
| oo | soon | balloon | school | noon | tool |
| | cool | smooth | goose | mood | choose |
| u, u_e | June | flume | usual | suing | tune |
| | flute | dues | glued | prunes | nude |
| | rude | bluish | truth | crude | jute |
| | bugle | prude | fluid | glucose | clues |
| u | numb | mustard | lunch | hunter | rusty |
| | trust | number | putter | butter | just |
| | thunder | hundred | punch | crust | bust |
| | budget | thumb | fudge | judge | lust |
| shwa a, e, o | cadet | thousand | balance | banana | balloon |
| | item | chapel | shovel | mitten | open |
| | beacon | honey | method | octopus | atom |

*The ESL Teacher's Book of Lists,* © 1993 by John Wiley & Sons, Inc.

# 5–9 PRACTICE FOR PHONEMES IN THE FINAL POSITION

## CONSONANTS

| English Spellings | Practice Words | | | | |
|---|---|---|---|---|---|
| b | stab | verb | carob | bulb | tub |
| | crib | nib | suburb | orb | bib |
| | drab | robe | bribe | globe | swab |
| | babe | slab | cob | cube | tube |
| c, k | back | crack | stack | stick | thick |
| | block | book | cake | hike | trick |
| | croak | smoke | coke | Mike | tack |
| | spike | truck | tuck | speak | trek |
| ch, tch | touch | breach | reach | clutch | catch |
| | ditch | pitch | much | inch | cinch |
| | punch | ranch | stench | stitch | itch |
| | couch | grouch | such | branch | ouch |
| d | dad | dead | deed | did | died |
| | dude | dud | wood | could | blood |
| | scold | around | code | shod | hound |
| | bland | brood | blade | dyed | breed |
| f | leaf | chief | off | brief | half |
| | proof | relief | safe | life | thief |
| | roof | laugh | fife | self | wolf |
| | muff | staff | rough | graph | goof |
| g | stag | flag | fig | sprig | bag |
| | log | hug | drug | brig | slag |
| | frog | slug | fatigue | grog | fog |
| | beg | drag | league | flog | peg |
| j, g, dg | badge | sludge | fudge | cringe | rage |
| | large | surge | singe | edge | lunge |
| | bridge | hedge | pledge | wedge | barge |
| | lodge | purge | page | stage | ridge |
| l | keel | doll | pole | school | mile |
| | style | mole | dill | goal | shoal |
| | still | shale | smile | trill | tile |
| | kale | kennel | tunnel | title | trial |
| m | scream | drum | prom | swim | trim |
| | room | broom | loam | storm | some |
| | problem | cram | cream | crime | crumb |
| | stem | deem | inform | dome | slum |

149

| English Spellings | Practice Words | | | |
|---|---|---|---|---|
| n | learn | turn | tan | tine | torn |
| | corn | nine | stone | mine | moan |
| | grown | drown | sane | drain | tune |
| | spoon | dragon | plankton | mourn | phone |
| ng | sing | bang | tong | sung | bring |
| | sting | stung | song | lung | gang |
| p | scoop | drop | whip | swipe | drape |
| | ripe | limp | flip | crop | grope |
| | trap | lump | loop | pup | crape |
| | grape | pipe | ship | thump | troup |
| r | mirror | warrior | washer | flyer | error |
| | dear | over | editor | mayor | roar |
| | beer | fire | inspire | October | water |
| | stir | star | sire | sir | smear |
| s, c | trace | use | class | coarse | race |
| | juice | miss | abuse | bus | mice |
| | twice | boss | abyss | lass | loss |
| | truce | hearse | worse | curse | ice |
| sh | wish | cash | stash | gosh | blush |
| | mush | crush | dish | fish | frosh |
| | flash | trash | swish | posh | lush |
| | slush | flush | fresh | finish | mesh |
| t | habit | treat | skit | crate | write |
| | blot | foot | blunt | coat | quart |
| | stint | vote | flute | suit | shot |
| | fleet | edit | state | about | riot |
| th | tooth | twelfth | truth | booth | sleuth |
| v | sleeve | gave | give | slave | glove |
| | dove | cave | eve | Steve | love |
| | believe | twelve | stove | drive | move |
| | have | leave | wave | prove | five |
| z, s | clothes | froze | doze | shows | toes |
| | rose | graze | dresses | maze | farms |
| | firs | praise | eyes | years | hers |
| | flaws | dens | prize | rise | fleas |

# VOWELS

| English Spellings | Practice Words | | | |
|---|---|---|---|---|
| a, ay | ray | stray | clay | bay | quay |

| English Spellings | Practice Words | | | | |
|---|---|---|---|---|---|
| aw | saw | straw | claw | flaw | squaw |
| e, ee, ea, y | me | bee | tree | knee | he |
| | tiny | busy | flea | plea | silly |
| i, ie, igh, y | tie | lie | quasi | alumni | pie |
| | sty | sigh | sky | high | thigh |
| o, oe, ow | stow | go | snow | toe | mow |
| | blow | slow | hoe | hello | jello |
| oy | toy | boy | soy | coy | joy |
| u, ue, ew | mew | true | flue | clue | renew |
| | new | gnu | emu | crew | stew |

*crew*

## 5–10 *INTERNATIONAL PHONETIC ALPHABET AND ORTHOGRAPHIC EQUIVALENTS*

### CONSONANTS SOUNDS

| IPA Symbol | Orthographic Equivalents | Example |
|---|---|---|
| b | b | box |
| d | d | do |
| f | f | fast |
| g | g | gone |
| h | h | hat |
| k | k | book |
| l | l | lit |
| m | m | me |
| n | n | now |
| ŋ | ng | ring |
| p | p | pit |
| r | r | red |
| s | s | sit |
| ʃ | sh | shed |
| t | t | tack |
| θ | th | think |
| ð | *th* | they |
| v | v | vast |
| w | w | west |
| y | y | yet |
| z | z, s | zoo, rise |
| ʒ | s | treasure |
| tʃ | ch | cheat |
| dʒ | dg | fudge |

### VOWELS

| | | |
|---|---|---|
| a | o | hot |
| æ | a | hat |
| e | ā | ate |
| ɛ | e | met |
| i | ē | each |
| I | i | fit |
| ɔ | aw | saw |
| o | ō | hold |

| IPA Symbol | Orthographic Equivalents | Example |
|:---:|:---:|:---|
| u | o̅o̅ | soon |
| U | oo | foot |
| ə | u | but |
| ə | a, e, i, o, u | about |

## DIPHTHONGS

| | | |
|:---:|:---:|:---|
| aI | ī | tie |
| aU | ow | cow |
| ɔI | oi, oy, | boy |

# 5–11 *DICTIONARY PRONUNCIATION GUIDES*

Language learners frequently check dictionaries for the pronunciation and meaning of unfamiliar words. Reviewing these standard dictionary pronunciation guides will help.

| Key word | American Heritage | Funk & Wagnalls | Thorndike Barnhart |
|---|---|---|---|
| cat | ă | a | a |
| age | ā | ā | ā |
| care | â | â | ã |
| bar | ä | ä | ä |
| bit | b | b | b |
| chin | ch | ch | ch |
| did | d | d | d |
| let | ĕ | e | e |
| see | ē | ē | ē |
| fix | f | f | f |
| gas | ǵ | ǵ | ǵ |
| hat | h | h | h |
| pit | ĭ | i | i |
| tie | ī | ī | ī |
| pier | îr | | |
| judge | j | j | j |
| kiss | k | k | k |
| lip | l | l | l |
| mom | m | m | m |
| not | n | n | n |
| ring | ng | ng | ng |
| hot | ŏ | o | o |
| go | ō | ō | ō |
| saw | ô | ô | ô |
| boy | oi | oi | oi |
| out | ou | ou | ou |
| look | oŏ | oŏ | u̇ |
| fool | o͞o | o͞o | ū |
| pot | p | p | p |
| red | r | r | r |
| sis | s | s | s |
| she | sh | sh | sh |
| tip | t | t | t |
| think | th | th | th |
| the | *th* | th | ₸H |
| cut | ŭ | u | u |
| fur | ûr | ûr | ėr |
| vest | v | v | v |
| wed | w | w | w |

*The ESL Teacher's Book of Lists,* © 1993 by John Wiley & Sons, Inc.

| Key word | American Heritage | Funk & Wagnalls | Thorndike Barnhart |
|---|---|---|---|
| what | hw | hw | hw |
| yes | y | y | y |
| zest | z | z | z |
| treasure | zh | zh | zh |
| about | ə | ə | ə |
| terrible | ə | ə | ə |
| occur | ə | ə | ə |
| circus | ə | ə | ə |

# 5–12 ENGLISH STRESS AND INTONATION PATTERNS IN WORDS

**Stress** is the relative accent, emphasis, or degree of loudness placed on a syllable or word. In a word, the stress or accent is the result of pronouncing the word part slightly louder and/or longer than other parts of the word.

**Intonation** is the relative level of pitch in a spoken sentence. There are four speech pitches: below normal, normal, somewhat above normal, and very much above normal. Stress within a sentence occurs when words are pronounced at pitches above normal.

The regular patterns in speech caused by the position of stressed and unstressed syllables and by changes in intonation result in the characteristic **rhythm** of English.

## STRESS PATTERNS IN WORDS

1. Stress or accent is usually placed on the part of the word that carries the most meaning, such as the **base** or **root** in a polysyllabic word.

    EXAMPLE: *reWRITten.*

2. Prefixes and suffixes are usually not stressed.

    EXAMPLES: *unPLUGged, prePARE, TALKed, PORTable.*

3. Nouns, verbs, and adjectives of two or more syllables often are stressed on the first syllable, unless the first syllable is a prefix.

    EXAMPLES: *CHARacter, CELebrate, BEAUTiful.*

4. Stress is usually placed on the syllable **before** suffixes beginning with the letter *i*:

    | *ive* | *iant* | *ial* | *ic* | *ion* | *io* | *iate* |
    |-------|--------|-------|------|-------|------|--------|
    | *iar* | *ify*  | *ily* | *ish* | *iary* | *iable* | |

5. The first word in a compound word is usually stressed.

    EXAMPLES: *BANDstand, HEADset.*

## PRACTICE FOR STRESS PATTERNS IN WORDS

### WORDS WITH PREFIXES

| | | | |
|---|---|---|---|
| reWIND | unPAID | preDICT | exCEL |
| exHAUST | inCLUDE | inFECT | reWRITE |
| rePAINT | unHAPPY | unABLE | reMIND |
| deBATE | deFEND | overWHELM | overDUE |
| aSIDE | enCLOSE | prePARE | proTECT |

### WORDS WITH SUFFIXES

| | | | |
|---|---|---|---|
| SLOWly | FASTer | SPEAKing | AWful |
| FILTHy | SICKly | LOVEly | DRYing |

| | | | |
|---|---|---|---|
| BAKery | KINDness | HELPful | DRINKable |
| TALKing | TEACHer | ACTor | SERVant |
| SPEEDily | SMALLest | CAREless | LIFElike |

## WORDS WITH PREFIXES AND SUFFIXES

| | | | |
|---|---|---|---|
| unWORKable | imPOSSible | reFINing | deSCRIPtion |
| unCERTain | reMAINing | underSTANDing | reMARKable |
| unTIMEly | inCORRECTly | unREADable | reSPECTable |
| rePAYment | preSCRIPtion | inSISTant | inSPIRing |
| preDICTed | obSERVant | preHISTORic | unNATURal |

## POLYSYLLABIC WORDS

| | | | |
|---|---|---|---|
| RAdio | CARpenter | SENator | GASoline |
| POLitics | OCcupy | TENtative | HISTory |
| ALgebra | COUNtryman | STEReo | LABoratory |
| MASCuline | FEMinine | AGriculture | LIbrary |
| MINister | PRESident | CALendar | FURNiture |

## COMPOUND WORDS

| | | | |
|---|---|---|---|
| BASEball | NOTEbook | SIDEwalk | SNOWflake |
| DISHwasher | BRIEFcase | HAIRcut | WATERfall |
| TEXTbook | OUTfit | NEWSpaper | HEADache |
| TOOTHbrush | AIRport | POPcorn | SKATEboard |
| CLASSroom | HEADlight | OVERcoat | SKYlight |

## WORDS WITH "I" SUFFIXES

| | | | |
|---|---|---|---|
| dirECTive | inCENTive | reMEDial | cusTODial |
| biONic | oPINion | hisTORical | inCENDiary |
| ecoNOMics | neCESSity | comPANion | faMILiar |
| inSATiable | interMEDiary | eNORMity | scenERio |
| ofFICiate | doMINion | preVENTive | alLUVial |

*The ESL Teacher's Book of Lists,* © 1993 by John Wiley & Sons, Inc.

## 5–13 ENGLISH STRESS AND INTONATION PATTERNS IN SENTENCES

1. Content-bearing words (nouns, verbs, adjectives, and adverbs) are usually stressed, and function words (prepositions, conjunctions, articles, and pronouns) are not.

2. Words may be stressed for emphasis, as in: *NO, you may NOT go.*

3. The interrogative words—*who, what, where, when, why, and how*—are usually stressed in questions.

4. When one word in a sentence ends in a consonant sound and the next word begins with a vowel sound, the pause or juncture between the two words is reduced and the beginning vowel sound is weakened.

   For example, the sentence, "The fish are swimming," is pronounced, "The FISHer SWIMming." The stresses occur on the content words "fish" and "swim" but not on the article, the weakened verb, or the suffix.

5. When one word in a sentence ends with a vowel sound and the next word begins with a vowel sound, the juncture between the words is filled with a /w/ or /y/ sound.

   EXAMPLES: *See it.*    *Say it.*    *Sew it.*    *Do it.*
   See/y/it.    Say/y/it.    Sew/w/it.    Do/w/it.

6. PHONEMIC STRESS changes the meaning of the sentence. Consider the differences in meaning of this sentence when different elements of the sentence are stressed:

   *The GIRL lost the book.*
   *The girl LOST the book.*
   *The girl lost the BOOK.*

7. There are two basic intonation patterns for English sentences. The first is called Rising and Falling; the second is called Rising.

   *Rising and Falling*: In this pattern, the speaker's pitch gradually rises throughout the sentence and then falls on the last word. The falling pitch indicates the end of the sentence and is followed by the juncture between sentences.

   The Rising and Falling pattern is common for sentences that are simple statements, commands, or questions beginning with an interrogatory word.

   EXAMPLES: *I have a HEADache.*
   *Open the WINdow.*
   *Where are you GOing?*

   *Rising*: In this pattern, the speaker's pitch gradually rises throughout the sentence, ending in a higher-than-normal pitch. This pattern is common for questions requiring a yes or no answer, for tag-questions (that is, for questions consisting of a statement with an interrogatory phrase added at the end), or for direct address. In direct address, the rise in pitch occurs on the person's name, not on the title or other descriptive words.

*The ESL Teacher's Book of Lists,* © 1993 by John Wiley & Sons, Inc.

EXAMPLES:   *Is it TIME TO GO?*
*She didn't LEAVE, DID SHE?*
*Dr. SNOW, are you THERE?*

8.  Stress and intonation patterns may be practiced by mimicking Right to Left Strings or Left to Right Strings.

*Left to Right Strings*: Students listen and repeat the teacher's speech patterns as the teacher builds a sentence pattern by adding one word or phrase at a time from left to right, as in:

*I see.*

*I see a dog.*

*I see a big dog.*

*I see a big, black dog.*

*I see a big, black dog barking.*

*I see a big, black dog barking at the mailman.*

*Right to Left Strings*: Students listen and repeat the teacher's speech patterns as the teacher builds a sentence pattern by adding one word or phrase at a time from right to left, as in:

*park.*

*to the park.*

*going to the park.*

*He was going to the park.*

# SECTION 6
# Assessment

# 6–1 *LANGUAGE ASSESSMENT GUIDELINES*

A language assessment program is the basis for decision making about language students, curricula, and instructional resources. An assessment program also helps teachers and administrators measure the effectiveness of the language-education program. Different types of assessment instruments and tests are used for each of these functions. There are three types of assessment instruments: standardized tests, commercial nonstandardized tests, and teacher-made tests. The tests themselves are of many kinds.

The following chart shows the kind of instrument and test generally used for each assessment function.

| Assessment Function | Instrument Type | Test Type |
|---|---|---|
| **STUDENT DECISIONS** | | |
| Program eligibility | Standardized | Placement Test |
| | Standardized | Oral Interview |
| | Standardized | Achievement Test pretest |
| Exit standard | Standardized | Placement Test |
| | Standardized | Oral Interview |
| | Standardized | Achievement Test post-test |
| Instructional needs | Nonstandard | Diagnostic Test |
| | Nonstandard | Criterion-Referenced Test |
| | Nonstandard | Management Systems Test |
| | Nonstandard | Oral Interview |
| | Teacher-made | Criterion-Referenced Test |
| | Teacher-made | Observation w/checklist |
| | Teacher-made | Observation-worksamples |
| Learning Process | Standardized | Achievement Test |
| | Nonstandard | Criterion-Referenced Test |
| | Nonstandard | Management Systems Test |
| | Nonstandard | Oral Interview |
| | Teacher-made | Criterion-Referenced Test |
| | Teacher-made | Observation w/checklist |
| | Teacher-made | Observation-worksamples |
| **CURRICULUM DECISIONS*** | | |
| Language Program/ Students Match | Standardized | Achievement Test |
| | Nonstandard | Management Systems Test |
| | Nonstandard | Criterion-Referenced Test |
| | Teacher-made | Criterion-Referenced Test |

*Curriculum and program decisions should be based on class scores and profiles over time, not on individual students' scores.

| Assessment Function | Instrument Type | Test Type |
| --- | --- | --- |
| **CURRICULUM DECISIONS** (*continued*) | | |
| Language Program/ Regular Curriculum Match | Standardized Nonstandard Teacher-made | Achievement Test Management Systems Test Criterion-Referenced Test |
| **RESOURCE DECISIONS** | | |
| Instructional Time | Nonstandard Teacher-made | Management Systems Test Criterion-Referenced Test |
| Instructional Materials | Nonstandard Nonstandard Teacher-made Teacher-made | Diagnostic Test Criterion-Referenced Test Criterion-Referenced Test Observation-worksamples |
| **PROGRAM DECISIONS*** | | |
| Effectiveness | Standardized Standardized Nonstandard | Achievement Test Criterion-Referenced Test Management Systems Test |
| Pacing | Nonstandard Nonstandard | Management Systems Test Criterion-Referenced Test |

*The ESL Teacher's Book of Lists,* © 1993 by John Wiley & Sons, Inc.

*Curriculum and program decisions should be based on class scores and profiles over time, not on individual students' scores.

# 6–2 ASSESSING LANGUAGE PROFICIENCY

Language proficiency means communicating effectively in a target language using context-appropriate structures and content. This requires the integration of many individual pieces of language information including vocabulary, sound/symbol relationships, and grammar.

Use these integrative methods to assess students' language proficiency:

*Close Procedure for Written Passages*—Select a written passage of approximately 250 words. The passage may deal with functional, social/cultural, or curriculum content. Delete every fifth or seventh word. Direct students to read the passage silently and write in the missing words.

*Close Procedures for Aural Passages*—Select a passage of approximately 150 words. The passage may deal with functional, social/cultural, or curriculum content. Delete every fifth or seventh word. Present the passage to students, either by reading it aloud or by taping it with the deletions and directing them to listen to the tape. Ask students to select and mark the words that best complete the passage from choices provided on an answer sheet. As an alternative, provide a numbered answer sheet that corresponds to the number of deleted words. Ask students to supply appropriate words to complete the passage.

*Dictations*—Select a thematic passage of 100 to 150 words. Direct students to listen to the passage and then to write it verbatim. Read the passage three times: first, read it through at a conversational pace; next, read it slowly, breaking the passage into meaningful phrases of no more than five words each; and, finally, read it through at a moderate pace.

*Dramatizations by Individuals or Groups*—Select a topic for dramatization (See Thematic Language Units for suggestions). Prepare a script incorporating related vocabulary, gestures, movements, actions and props. Have student(s) learn the script and perform the dramatization for the class. Intermediate or advanced students may also be asked to develop the script or may be asked to do an extemporaneous dramatization on a given topic.

*Formula Dialogues*—Create a set of cue cards that present different social or functional language situations, for example, asking for directions to the supermarket or introducing your friend Tom to Uncle Chuck. Direct pairs of students to pick a card from the set and engage in the cued formula dialogue.

*Listen and Respond*—Select a passage of 200 to 250 words and tape record it or read it aloud to the students. Direct students to listen to the passage and then answer open-ended questions about the content or meaning of the text. As an alternative, direct students to write the answers to the questions or to write a summary of the passage.

*Read/Listen and Respond*—Select a passage of 200 to 250 words. Direct students either to read the passage or to listen to it as it is read aloud or presented on tape and then respond to multiple-choice questions. Use all combinations of presentation and response modes: written text and aural/oral questions and answers; aural text and aural/oral questions and answers; written text and written questions and answers; aural text and written questions and answers.

*Prepared Narrative*—Ask students to research a self-selected or assigned topic and prepare an oral presentation of between 3 to 7 minutes. Encourage the use of visual aids, including charts and graphs.

*Paraphrase Recognition*—Select passages of between 100 and 150 words each and develop paraphrased passages of varying quality for each passage. Ask students to select the best paraphrase for the material from the choices given. Use all combinations of presentation and response modes: aural material/aural choices; aural material/written choices; written material/aural choices; written material/written choices.

*Story Retelling*—Ask students to read or listen to a story of between 200 and 250 words, then retell the story. The stories should have functional, social/cultural, or curricular content. Gist recall, not verbatim, is required.

*Storytelling*—Ask students to prepare, then tell a story, either factual or fiction.

*Structured Interview*—Interview students, using a prepared set of questions on target topics. Develop a checklist of language features to note in the students' responses.

*Translations*—Direct students to translate written passages of varying lengths from their native language into English. The passages may deal with functional, social/cultural, or curriculum content.

*The ESL Teacher's Book of Lists*, © 1993 by John Wiley & Sons, Inc.

# 6–3  *ASSESSING AUDITORY/AURAL SKILLS*

Auditory skills refer to the ability of the ear to hear meaningful sounds. In language learning, auditory skills include the trained or culturally acquired ability to recognize the sounds that belong to a particular language and the ability to discriminate among similar sounds within the language. Aural skills refer to the ability of the student to listen to and understand spoken messages.

## I. USE THESE METHODS TO ASSESS STUDENTS' AUDITORY SKILLS:

*Sound Contrast Recognition in Words*—Ask students to listen carefully as you read groups of two or three words aloud. Tell them to indicate whether the words in the groups are the same or different by circling "same" or "different" (S/D) on their answer sheets. Use minimal contrasts. Examples: *sit/set; sit/sit/sit; set/sit/sit.*

*Sound Contrast Recognition in Sentences*—Ask students to listen carefully as you read pairs of sentences aloud. Tell them to indicate whether the pairs are the same or different by writing or circling "same" or "different" (S/D) on their answer sheets. Use minimal contrasts. Example: *Did she get it? / Did she pet it?*

*Target Sound Discrimination in Word Pairs*—Tell students to listen carefully to the initial sound of the word you are about to say, then to listen to pairs of words. Ask them to write or circle "yes" or "no" (Y/N) on their answer sheets to indicate whether the pairs of words have the same initial sound as the target word. Use the same method for medial and final sounds.

*Target Sound Discrimination in Word Groups*—Tell students to listen carefully to the initial sound of the word you are about to say, then to listen to the initial sound in each of the next four words. Ask them to indicate whether the other words have the same initial sound as the target word. Example: *bit—Ben, bug, pit, bat.* Students may respond by writing or circling "yes" or "no" (Y/N), by raising their hands when the initial sounds are the same, or by holding up a card that says "same" or "different." Use this method to assess sound recognition in the final and medial positions also.

*The ESL Teacher's Book of Lists,* © 1993 by John Wiley & Sons, Inc.

*Rhyming Word Recognition*—Ask students to listen carefully to the ending sounds as you read pairs of words and to write or circle "yes" or "no" (Y/N) on their answer sheet to indicate whether the pairs rhyme.

*Sound/Spelling Association and Recognition*—Direct students to listen to word parts, words, word pairs, or word groups as you read them aloud. Tell students to circle the matching items on their answer sheets. Prepare multiple-choice answer sheets with four choices.

*Sound/Spelling Association and Production*—Direct students to listen to the words you will read aloud, then to write the words. Begin by using words with target sounds presented in initial position, then the medial and final positions.

*Sound/Spelling Discrimination*—Ask students to listen as you read a series of three words aloud, then, on an answer sheet with four words per item, to cross out the word they did not hear. The exercise can also be done using word parts, word pairs, or phrases.

## II. USE THESE METHODS TO ASSESS STUDENTS' AURAL SKILLS:

*Vocabulary*—Direct students to listen as you read a word, then to mark the matching picture on their answer sheets.

*Aural Understanding/Pictorial Match*—Direct students to listen as you read a short passage, then to mark the picture on the answer sheet that matches the passage just read. Begin with simple noun phrases *(the happy baby)* and verb phrases *(hit the ball)*. Repeat the exercise with simple sentences, followed by brief passages of up to five sentences.

*Aural Comprehension/Sentence Completion*—Direct students to listen as you read the beginning of a sentence and a set of possible endings. Ask students to indicate on their answer sheet which of the endings best completes the sentence. Provide four choices.

*Aural Understanding of Main Idea or Gist*—Select a passage of between 100 and 200 words. Direct students to listen to the passage, then to select the best title for the passage from choices you will read to them. As an alternative, ask students to select the main idea or gist statement from the choices orally or visually presented on an answer sheet.

*Aural Comprehension to Complete a Task*—Direct students to listen carefully and to follow your directions. Begin with a single, but specific, task *(raise your right hand)*, then move on to a sequence of steps for the completion of a task.

*Simon Says*—Play Simon Says and incorporate key direction vocabulary *(first, second, left, right, up, down, in, on, close, open,* and so forth) in Simon's orders. Winners may serve as Simons for subsequent rounds of play.

*The ESL Teacher's Book of Lists,* © 1993 by John Wiley & Sons, Inc.

*Logical Predictions*—Select a passage of between 150 and 250 words. Ask students to listen to the passage and three additional statements, then to select the statement that best tells what is most likely to happen next in the story.

*Paraphrase Recognition*—Select brief passages of up to 150 words and construct three single sentence paraphrases for each. Direct students to listen as you read each passage and three statements. Ask them to select the statement that is closest in meaning to the passage.

*Factual Understanding*—Ask students to listen as you read a set of brief statements. Tell them to indicate on their answer sheets whether each statement is true or false (T/F).

*Logical Understanding*—Direct students to listen carefully as you read a statement containing an error. Tell students to give or write the correction for the statement. Example: *Eli slept in his book (bed).*

# 6–4 ASSESSING READING COMPREHENSION

Use these methods to assess students' reading comprehension:

*Close Procedure for Comprehension*—Select a written passage of approximately 250 words that deals with functional, social/cultural, or curriculum content. Delete every fifth or seventh word. Ask students to read the passage and to fill in the missing words. As an easier alternative, direct students to fill in the missing words from choices presented on the answer sheet.

*Coherence Recognition*—Create written passages in which you embed words, phrases, and/or sentences that do not fit the meaning of the whole. Direct students to read the passages and to circle the misfit words, phrases, or sentences.

*Gist Recognition*—Select a passage of between 100 and 200 words. Ask students to read the passage, then to select the best title, main-idea statement, or summary statement for the passage. Provide four choices for each item.

*Logical Predictions from Reading*—Select written passages of between 150 and 250 words. Direct students to read each passage and its four additional statements, then to select a statement that best represents the most likely next occurrence for each passage.

*Paraphrase Recognition*—Select a passage of up to 200 words and create four related statements, one of which is a paraphrase of the passage. Direct students to read the passage and statements and to select the one that best paraphrases the passage.

*Factual Comprehension*—Select a written passage of between 200 and 250 words. Prepare a set of detail or factual questions related to the passage. Direct students to read the passage and questions and to select answers from the choices provided.

*Inferential Comprehension*—Select a written passage of between 200 and 250 words. Prepare a set of inference or analytical questions relating to the passage. Direct students to read the passage and questions and to select answers from the choices provided.

# 6–5  *ASSESSING ORAL LANGUAGE SKILLS*

To adequately assess oral language skills evaluate both kinds of oral language: one-way speech and interactive speech. In one-way speech, the speaker addresses an audience as in a formal presentation or lecture, and there is little, if any, expected reply. During interactive speech, each speaker reacts to the other, guiding or changing the conversation accordingly. Interactive speech is the most common type of oral communication.

Use these methods for assessing students' oral language skills:

*Taped Improvement Records*—At the beginning of an instructional program, course, or semester, tape record all students individually as they state their names, state the date of the recording, read a prepared target-level passage, and tell a story on an assigned topic. At intervals during the instructional program, follow the same procedure, using the same passage and assigned topic. Compare progress over time. Permit students to review their tapes and to make a personal assessment of growth.

*Self-Assessment*—Interview students and ask them to respond to assessment questions such as these:

*Do you feel at ease and confident when speaking English*

- *with classmates and friends?*
- *When speaking English in stores? At the bank? At your job? In your ESL class? In other classes?*

*Can you usually follow and respond in a conversation*

- *when one person is speaking to you? When two or more people are speaking to you? When people are talking, but not just to you?*

*Can you usually understand what is being said by people*

- *talking on TV? On the radio? On the telephone? On a public-address system?*

*Do you usually know the right words to use when*

- *speaking to someone at the bank? At your school? In the grocery store? At the doctor's office? At a party? At a job interview? At the train station or airport? At the gasoline service station?*

*Giving Directions*—Have a student give directions orally to another student for the completion of a simple assigned task, such as making a sandwich. Intermediate or advanced students may give directions for tasks requiring the use of technical or advanced vocabulary and multiple steps, such as mixing a solution for a science class.

*Extemporaneous Narrative*—Direct the student to select from a set of topic cards and to prepare a brief oral presentation. Allow five minutes of preparation for a three-minute narrative; ten minutes of preparation for a five- to seven-minute narrative. Students may make and use an outline or brief notes.

*Twenty Questions*—Prepare sets of twenty questions on single topics and ask individual students to respond to each. Use a moderate pace for the question-and-answer protocol and vary the types of questions asked (*yes/no, tag, open-ended, negative, opinion, comparison*, and so forth).

*Paired Discussion*—Direct pairs of students to discuss an event or situation. You may provide a photo as a stimulus. No preparation time is permitted.

*Paired Decision Making*—Direct pairs of students to engage in a discussion that leads to making a decision. For example, provide the pair with newspaper ads for three stereo systems and ask them to discuss the features and prices of each and to determine the best buy.

*Impromptu Storytelling*—Direct students to prepare, then to tell a story. The story should be original and creative. Encourage the use of gestures, movement, and props.

*Cued Storytelling*—Have students select a story cue card showing an event in progress. Tell them to describe what is happening in the picture and then to make up and relate a suitable ending for the story.

*Oral Report*—Direct students to research a self-selected or assigned topic and to prepare a presentation of between three and seven minutes. Encourage the use of visual aids, including charts and graphs. Advanced students should speak on a complex situation or idea.

*Open-Ended Interview*—Interview each student individually for ten to twenty minutes. Ask leading questions and provide continuation prompts so the conversation is extended and permits at least some topics to be exhausted before moving on to new ones.

*Structured Interview*—Interview each student individually using a prepared set of questions on target subjects. This is especially useful to assess vocabulary related to specific subjects or situations.

*Role Play*—Direct pairs of students to role play on assigned topics. For example, one student asks the other for advice on selecting an affordable restaurant.

*Dramatization*—Select a topic for dramatization and direct a small group of students to prepare a script incorporating dialogue, gestures, movement, and props. Have the students practice and perform the dramatization.

*Reading Aloud*—Select passages of various types (*narrative, instructive, poetry, technical*) and have individual students read them aloud.

*The ESL Teacher's Book of Lists,* © 1993 by John Wiley & Sons, Inc.

***Poetry***—Have students prepare and recite poetry, rhymes, or riddles aloud to the class.

***Story Retelling***—Direct individual students to listen to a tape-recorded story of between 200 and 250 words, then to retell the story in their own words. Gist recall, not verbatim recall, is required.

# 6–6  *ASSESSING WRITTEN LANGUAGE SKILLS*

Written language proficiency has two components: vocabulary and structure. The more extensive the students' vocabulary, the better able they will be to express their ideas. Structure refers to grammar, punctuation, and other rules.

## I. USE THESE METHODS TO ASSESS STUDENTS' VOCABULARY:

*Definition*—Show students pictures from a set of target objects or concepts and have them write the name and a definition for each picture. This exercise can be used with advanced content-subject vocabulary as well as with the most basic concepts. As examples, create a set of pictures that shows lab equipment, cell-division sequences, or molecular structure, or create a set of pictures showing basic items of clothing.

*Vocabulary Matching*—Give students a set of pictures of objects or concepts and a set of words that name each picture. Direct students to match the pictures with the correct words.

*Naming*—Direct students to write the appropriate vocabulary word when shown pictures or visual representations of the word.

*Classifying Concepts*—Ask students to arrange into meaningful categories words presented on flash cards, then to copy the words on paper and to label each category. Use 20 to 30 flash cards at a time. For example: (transportation words) *car, bus, train, bike, skateboard;* (words that describe people) *happy, angry, tired, old, thin;* (job titles) *waiter, teacher, baker, teller, priest;* (buildings) *school, theater, post office, deli, factory.*

*Distinguishing Meaningful Categories*—Give students a worksheet on which words are presented in groups of five, including one word that does not share the relationship of the other four. Have students cross out the words that do not belong and replace them with appropriate words.

*Matching Definitions*—Prepare a worksheet with target words listed in the left column and their definitions listed in a different order in the right column. Have students match the words to their correct definitions.

*Multiple-Choice Definitions*—Prepare a worksheet with target words presented with four possible definitions. Have students select and circle the correct definitions.

*Recognizing Antonyms and Synonyms*—Prepare a worksheet in which the target words are presented and paired with another word, either an antonym or a synonym. Have students indicate by writing "A" or "S" on the worksheet whether the pairs are antonyms or synonyms.

*The ESL Teacher's Book of Lists,* © 1993 by John Wiley & Sons, Inc.

*Supplying Antonyms and Synonyms*—Have students write either antonyms or synonyms for a set of target words listed on a worksheet.

*Analogies*—Direct students to fill in the missing word in a series of analogies. Vary the difficulty of the analogy format. Test knowledge of part/whole; antonyms; synonyms; cause/effect; size; use; and so forth.

*Close Procedure for Vocabulary*—Select a passage of 200 to 250 words and delete target words, either specific vocabulary or word types. Direct students to fill in the missing words in the passage.

*Interpreting Idioms*—Provide students with a list of idioms and idiomatic expressions and ask them to provide paraphrases of the meaning.

*Vocabulary Editing*—Provide a worksheet of sentences containing target vocabulary words used either correctly or incorrectly with respect to the meaning of the words. Have students "edit" the incorrect usage by changing the word or changing the context.

*Multiple-Meaning Words*—Provide students with a list of multiple-meaning words (homonyms). Direct them to write sets of sentences that show the correct use of each word in its various contexts.

*Using Context Clues*—Select a passage of 200 to 250 words and replace key words with nonsense syllables. Direct students to read the passage and replace the nonsense words with appropriate words.

*Semantic Mapping*—Provide students with sets of related words and have them create semantic maps showing the relationships among the words.

## II. USE THESE METHODS TO ASSESS STUDENTS' KNOWLEDGE OF LANGUAGE STRUCTURE:

*Sentence Order*—Select ten sentences of appropriate difficulty for the students. Take the words of each sentence and rewrite them in a randomly ordered list, removing punctuation and capitalization. Give students the lists and have them re-create the sentences with proper word order, punctuation, and capitalization.

*Close Procedure for Grammar*—Select a passage of 150 words and delete words that fit a grammatical type, such as possessive pronouns. Have students complete the passage by writing in the missing words. Example: *Arthur, Jill and John gave the girl _____ coats.*

*Editing*—Develop a written passage of 150 to 200 words that includes embedded errors in grammar, spelling, punctuation, word order, and capitalization. Direct students to edit the passage, correcting all errors.

*Embedded Choice*—Develop a written passage of 200 to 250 words that includes several embedded choices focused on grammar or mechanics. Have students cross out the incorrect words so that the final version of the passage is coherent and correct. Example: *Jack and John took (his/their) books to the library. (They/We) gave (it/them) to the librarian.*

*Expansion*—Develop a written passage of 200 to 250 words that includes several embedded word cues. Direct students to insert suitable words into the passage according to the cues. Example: *The (adjective, adjective) man walked (adverb) (preposition) the barn.*

*Variations on a Theme*—Select a passage of approximately 100 words. Direct students to rewrite the passage to change the voice from active to passive; change the tense from past to future; change the subject from third person to first person plural, and so forth. Some basic passages can be used to test all standard transformations.

*Literal Translations*—Give students passages in their native languages and ask them to translate them into standard American English. Select brief passages on a variety of topics so that different grammatical patterns and vocabulary are required.

*Registers*—Direct students to rewrite a passage to change the register to suit a specific audience. For example, have students rewrite a compliment so that it is suitable for a four-year-old sister; a priest, rabbi or other clergy; a policeman; a best friend.

*Essays*—Have students select topics and develop a thesis statement for the topic. Then have the students draft, edit, and produce final versions of their essays.

*The ESL Teacher's Book of Lists,* © 1993 by John Wiley & Sons, Inc.

# 6–7 COMMERCIAL LANGUAGE TESTS

**Bahia Oral Language Test (BOLT), 1977**
Cohen, S. et al.
Measure of oral English and/or Spanish syntax, simple to complex, for intermediate and above

> Bahia, Inc.
> P.O. Box 9337
> North Berkeley Station
> Berkeley, CA 94709

**Bilingual Syntax Measure (BSM), 1975**
Burt, Marina K. et al.
Measure of oral syntatic proficiency in English and/or Spanish

> The Psychological Corporation
> 555 Academic Court
> San Antonio, TX 78204-0952

**Bilingual Syntax Measure II (BSM)**
Test Development Department, Harcourt Brace Jovanovich, Inc.
Measure of oral syntatic proficiency in English or Spanish using elementary through high school students' elicited speech

> Test Department
> Harcourt Brace Jovanovich, Inc.
> 757 Third Avenue
> New York, NY 10017

**Boehm Test of Basic Concepts (BTBD), 1971**
Boehm, Ann.
Group-administered elementary-level test of spatial and other concepts considered necessary for school achievement

> The Psychological Corporation
> 555 Academic Court
> San Antonio, TX 78204-0952

**Comprehensive English Language Test for Speakers of English as a Second Language (CELT)**
Palmer, Leslie & Harris, David
Group-administered multiple-choice measure of intermediate through adult English language proficiency with subtests in listening, structure, and vocabulary

> McGraw-Hill International Book Company
> 330 West 42nd Street
> New York, NY 10036

**Comprehensive Test of Basic Skills (CTBS), 1974**
CTB/McGraw-Hill
Group-administered multiple-choice measure of proficiency in reading, language mechanics, spelling, and mathematics, K–12; English and Spanish

> CTB/McGraw-Hill
> 8301 Ambassador Row
> Dallas, TX 75247

**Dailey Language Facility Test**
Dailey, J. T.
Rates oral language facility for elementary students by grading oral responses to pictures

> The Allington Corporation
> 801 North Pitt Street #707
> Alexandria, VA 22314

**Degrees of Reading Power**
The College Board
Group-administered cloze test of prose reading comprehension for elementary through adult; English and Spanish

> The College Board
> 888 Seventh Avenue
> New York, NY 10106

**Diagnostic Test for Students of English as a Secondary Language**
Davis, A. L.
Group-administered multiple-choice test of English structure and idiomatic vocabulary for intermediate through adult students

> Webster/McGraw-Hill Company
> 1221 Avenue of the Americas
> New York, NY 10036

**English as a Second Language Placement Test (EPT)**
Ilyin, Donna
Group-administered multiple-choice grammar tests, intermediate through adult; English

> Donna Ilyin
> Alemany Adult School
> 750 Eddy Street
> San Francisco, CA 94109

**English Language Test for Foreign Students**
University of Michigan
Group-administered written test of grammar, vocabulary, and reading comprehension for intermediate through adult learners of English

> English Language Institute
> University of Michigan
> 2001 N. University
> Ann Arbor, MI 48109

### Henderson-Moriarty ESL Literacy Placement Test
### (HELP)

Henderson, C. & Moriarty, P.

Placement test with subtests for oral, reading, and writing skills

Alemany Press
A Division of Janus Book Publishers
2501 Industrial Parkway West
Hayward, CA 94545

### Idea Oral Language Proficiency Tests
### (IPT I & II)

Dalton, E. et al.

Measures vocabulary, comprehension, syntax, and verbal expression including articulation of elementary through secondary school students; proficiency and diagnostic uses; English and Spanish

Ballard & Tighe, Inc.
480 Atlas Street
Brea, CA 92621

### Ilyin Oral Interview Test

Ilyin, Donna

Structured individual oral interview from simple to complex items for intermediate and adult students of English

Newbury House Publishers, Inc.
68 Middle Road
Rowley, MA 01969

### Language Assessment Battery
### (LAB)

New York City Board of Education

Group-administered (one individual section), assessment of reading, writing, listening comprehension and speaking for elementary through adult students; English and Spanish

Riverside Publishing Company
1919 South Highland Avenue
Lombard, IL 60148

### Language Assessment Scales
### (LAS)

DeAvila, E. A. & Duncan, S. E.

Individual test of English phoneme production, sound discrimination, listening comprehension, speaking, and pragmatic language use for elementary through adult students

Linguametrics Group
P.O. Box 454
Corte Madiera, CA 94925

**Language Proficiency Test**
> Gerard, J. & Weinstock, G.
> Placement and diagnostic test with aural/oral, reading, and writing subtests for intermediate and high school students

> > Academic Therapy Publishers
> > 20 Commercial Boulevard
> > Novado, CA 94947-6191

**MLA Cooperative Foreign Language Tests**
> Educational Testing Service & Modern Language Association
> Group audiolingual method tests for assessing the functional language of intermediate through college learners of French, German, Italian, Russian, and Spanish

> > Addison-Wesley Publishing Co., Inc.
> > 2527 Sand Hill Road
> > Menlo Park, CA 94025

**The Maculaitis Assessment Program MAC:K–12**
> Maculaitis, Jean D'Arcy
> Individual or group-administered multipurpose test for elementary through adult learners; diagnostic, placement, pre-post program criteria; skills areas: listening, speaking, reading, vocabulary, and writing

> > Alemany Press
> > A Division of Janus Book Publishers
> > 2501 Industrial Parkway West
> > Hayward, CA 94545

**Secondary Level English Proficiency Test (SLEP)**
> Educational Testing Service
> Local-administered and scored group test of overall English proficiency (listening comprehension, grammar, vocabulary and reading comprehension) for intermediate and secondary students

> > Educational Testing Service
> > Box 6155
> > Princeton, NJ 08541-6155

**Sequential Tests of Educational Progress (STEP)**
**Series III**
> Educational Testing Service
> Multiple-choice achievement test for elementary through high school students in reading, vocabulary, writing, math, science, social science, study skills, and listening

> > CTB/McGraw-Hill
> > 8301 Ambassador Row
> > Dallas, TX 75247

*The ESL Teacher's Book of Lists,* © 1993 by John Wiley & Sons, Inc.

**Speaking Proficiency English Assessment Kit**
**(SPEAK)**
>   Educational Testing Service
>   Individual assessment of oral proficiency for advanced secondary and college students, graduate teaching assistants, and teachers

>>   Educational Testing Service
>>   Box 6155
>>   Princeton, NJ 08541-6155

**Structure Test for the English Language**
**(STEL)**
>   Newbury House Publishers
>   Group-administered beginning through advanced level tests of English language structure for placement/pre-post assessment

>>   Newbury House Publishers
>>   68 Middle Road
>>   Rowley, MA 01969

**Test of Aural Comprehension**
>   Lado, Robert
>   Group test of aural comprehension; pick the picture that matches the passage heard; intermediate through adult students

>>   English Language Institute
>>   University of Michigan
>>   2001 N. University
>>   Ann Arbor, MI 48109

**Test of English as a Foreign Language**
**(TOEFL)**
>   Educational Testing Service
>   Group-administered proficiency assessment for college admissions and placement at national test sites

>>   Educational Testing Service
>>   Box 6155
>>   Princeton, NJ 08541-6155

**Test of English Proficiency Level**
>   Rathmell, George
>   Criterion-referenced placement test for intermediate through adult students; four skill areas: oral, structure, reading, and writing

>>   Alemany Press
>>   A Division of Janus Book Publishers
>>   2501 Industrial Parkway West
>>   Hayward, CA 94545

**Test of Spoken English (TSE)**

Educational Testing Service
Measures overall comprehensibility, pronunciation, grammar, and fluency of advanced students, adults, professionals

> Educational Testing Service
> Box 6155
> Princeton, NJ 08541-6155

**Test of Written English (TWE)**
Educational Testing Service
Measures English writing skills for college admissions; 30-minute essay; holistic scoring

> Educational Testing Service
> Box 6155
> Princeton, NJ 08541-6155

**The Second Language Oral Test of English**
Fathman, Ann K.
Diagnostic/placement measure for twenty syntactical structures for beginning- and intermediate-level students

> Alemany Press
> A Division of Janus Book Publishers
> 2501 Industrial Parkway West
> Hayward, CA 94545

**Woodcock Language Proficiency Battery**, 1980
Woodcock, Richard
Individually administered test measuring oral language, reading, and written language of elementary through adult learners; English and Spanish forms

> DLM
> P.O. Box 4000
> One DLM Park
> Allen, TX 75002

*The ESL Teacher's Book of Lists,* © 1993 by John Wiley & Sons, Inc.

# SECTION 7
# Curriculum and Instruction

# 7–1  THEMATIC LANGUAGE UNITS

This list will help you plan vocabulary lessons, choose topics for dialogues, identify areas to test for students' situational proficiencies, develop comprehensive instructional programs, provide ideas for cross-cultural research and discussions, and suggest ideas for students' homework or class projects.

**Animals**

Types of animals
Habitats of animals
Pets
Common pet names
Zoos

**Civic responsibility**

Divisions of government
Law and safety
Elections and voting
Police, fire, and other services
Municipal buildings

**Education**

Types of schools
Classroom vocabulary
Content subject vocabulary
School-related vocabulary and idioms

**Employment**

Types of jobs
Reading a want ad
Interviews
Résumés
Office life
Work routines
Benefits and rules
Business correspondence: letters, memos, reports
Filling out applications and other forms

**Family**

Names for family members
Relationships
Roles in the family

**Food**

Names of food
Names of meals

185

**Food (*continued*)**

Food preparation and recipe vocabulary
Kitchen and table items
Grocery shopping
Going to a restaurant

**Grooming**

Going to the hairdresser
Going to the barber
Cosmetics and grooming aids
Idioms and vocabulary of personal grooming

**Health**

Body parts
Illnesses, medical terms
Medicines, pharmacy terms
Doctors and dentists
Medical tests and procedures
Making an appointment with a doctor
Hospitals and emergency-care centers
Dealing with emergencies

**Housing**

Types of housing
Reading a newspaper ad for an apartment or house
Terms of purchase or lease
Reading/understanding a lease
Addresses/mail

**Measurement**

Sizes
Quantities
Distances
Measurement tools and equipment

**Money and banking**

Opening bank accounts
Applying for credit cards
Applying for loans

**Numbers**

Ordinal
Cardinal
Number formats: decimal, fractions, etc.
Numbers we use: phone, social security, ID's

*The ESL Teacher's Book of Lists,* © 1993 by John Wiley & Sons, Inc.

**Passage of time**

> Time vocabulary
> Instruments of time measurement
> Days of the week
> Months of the year
> Seasons
> Holidays
> Time idioms and formula dialogues

**Repairs**

> Tradesmen (electricians, carpenters, etc.)
> Common household problems
> Common tools and supplies
> Common shop vocabulary
> Contracts

**Shopping**

> Places to shop
> Clothing and accessories
>> Names of clothing and accessories
>> Care of clothing
>> Fabrics
>> Styles
> Colors
> Shopping idioms and vocabulary

**Social**

> Greetings
> Making introductions
> Terms of respect
> Etiquette
> Hospitality and visiting
> Gestures
> Entertainment and leisure activities
>> Art
>> Music/radio
>> Movies/television/video
>> Dancing
>> Games
>> Libraries
>> Museums/galleries
>> Newspapers, magazines, books
> Friendship/dating
> Using the phone
> Giving and receiving gifts
> Social letter writing

**Sports and hobbies**

Names of sports
Sports equipment and uniforms
Sports locations
Sporting events
Sport teams and activities
Names of hobbies
Hobby equipment
Hobby activities, associations, events
Specialized sports vocabulary
Sports-related active verbs
Sports-related idioms and formula dialogues
Hobby-related active verbs
Hobby-related idioms and formula dialogues

**Transportation**

Modes of transportation/travel
Asking for directions
Following directions/maps
Hotels/motels
States and capitals, other place names
Car/driving
  Car types and parts vocabulary
  Car travel vocabulary
  Car repair vocabulary
  Highway signs and symbols
  Getting a driver's license/registration
  Getting car insurance
Trains/buses
  Train and bus vocabulary
  Reading train and bus schedules
  Buying tickets
Airplanes/ships
  Airplane and ship vocabulary
  Reading air and ship timetables
  Buying tickets
  Passports/visas/customs
Other transportation
  Subway systems
  Bicycles/motorcycles
  Carpools

**Weather**

Weather conditions
Ranges of similar weather conditions
Weather-related activities, clothing, shelter
Weather idioms and formula dialogues

# 7–2  ACTIVITIES FOR DEVELOPING AUDITORY SKILLS

*Sound Flash*—Ask students to listen carefully to the beginning sound of the word you are about to say, then to listen to the beginning sounds of other words. Have students hold up either a "yes" or a "no" response flashcard after each word to show whether it has the same beginning sound as the target word. Example: *dig-dad, bed, dark, dinner.* After students can recognize the target sound in the initial position, repeat the activity for the sound in the final and medial positions.

*Sound Switch*—Ask students to pay attention to the beginning sounds of a series of words that you will read to them. Direct them to raise their hands when they notice that you "switched" to a word that begins with a different sound. Read at least four words with the same sound before introducing one with a different initial sound.

*Same or Different?*—Ask students to listen as you read pairs of words and to indicate whether the two words are the same or different. Students may respond orally or by holding up "same" or "different" flashcards. Train students' auditory discrimination by beginning with gross differences and working down to minimal pairs. For example: *house/hat, pin/bin.*

*Imposter*—Have students listen as you say groups of three words, two of which are the same, one which differs by only one sound. Ask students to show which word was different by holding up a flashcard with the number 1, 2, or 3 on it. Example: *pat, pit, pit. (1)*

*Repeat After Me*—Present a target sound in isolation, then as the initial sound in a word. Have students listen and repeat the sequence. Continue the exercise with several words for each target sound. Examples: /p/ *Pete;* /p/ *pet;* /p/ *pack;* /p/ *pitch.*

*Rhyme Time*—First have students listen to and repeat pairs of rhyming words; then have students suggest additional words that rhyme with the pairs.

*Speed Recognition Game*—The object of the game is to hear the target initial sound each time it is used. Scores represent the number of times students "missed" the word. Zero is a perfect score. To play, announce the target sound, then read a list of twenty-five words with the target sound words randomly interpersed. Read at a moderately fast pace. Students may make hatch marks on paper to keep track. Keep students' scores and challenge them to improve when the game is played again.

*Hide and Seek*—Present a target sound and groups of three words, one of which contains the target sound in the initial, medial, or final position. Ask students to indicate which word has the target sound by circling the number 1, 2, or 3 on an answer sheet. Examples: /t/ *by, tie, lie (2);* /t/ *wait, wade, wake (1).*

***Close Calls***—Give students a worksheet of word pairs for problem contrasts. Have students listen as you read one of the paired words and have them circle it on the worksheet. Examples: *they/day - day; then/den - then.*

***Starts with***—In a rapidly paced exchange, say a word aloud and have students respond with the letter used to spell the initial sound of the word. Repeat the activity for the final sounds.

***Flash Spell***—Give students sets of flashcards on which are printed the spellings of sounds. Direct students to hold up the card that spells the sound they hear at the beginning, end, or in the middle of the words you will read.

***Spell/Write Bee***—Read a list of words aloud and have students write them. Give up to thirty words to review five sound/spelling correspondences in an exercise. Repeat the exercise by having individual students spell the words orally.

# 7–3 *ACTIVITIES FOR DEVELOPING AURAL SKILLS*

*Pick a Pic*—Direct students to listen to the word that you will say and to mark the picture on the answer sheet that shows the item named. Use words that target sounds learned and require auditory discrimination of contrasts. Example: *man/pan; hat/bat; sun/run.*

*Class Keys*—Direct students to listen to the directions that you will give and to follow them on the answer sheet. Introduce school-related vocabulary by demonstrating each action on the chalkboard or overhead projector screen. Examples: *Put an X . . . , Underline the . . . , Draw a line . . . , Connect . . . , Circle the . . . , Fill in the space below . . . .*

*Show Me a Pen*—Give students sets of 12 concept cards that show pictures of words having problem contrasts, for example, a lamp/a ramp, a lake/a rake. Direct students to arrange the concept cards face up on the desk and ask them to point to or pick up the picture of the objects you say. Tell students to "show me a _____," filling in the names of the pictured objects.

*Simon Says*—Play the children's game "Simon Says," eliminating children from the game as they make errors following the directions. Use the game to teach parts of the body, items of clothing, position words, action verbs, gesture words, and expression words.

*Captions*—Ask students to listen as you read a sentence, then to mark the picture on their answer sheets that matches the sentence. Examples: pictures depict *a girl petting a dog and a girl feeding a dog.* Sentences: *Mary pet the dog. Mary fed the dog.*

*Happy Endings*—Direct students to listen as you read the beginning part of a sentence and possible endings. Tell students to indicate on their answer sheets which of the endings best completes the sentence. Provide four choices. Begin with simple sentences and one-word completers, then go to more complex sentences. Example: *Tom hit the _____. chair, book, ball, key*

*What's It All About?*—Direct students to listen as you read them a story. Read a brief passage of five sentences, then ask students to listen and to pick from four choices the word that best tells the topic of the passage. Students mark the corresponding number on their answer sheets.

*Van Gogh?*—Tell students to follow your directions and to complete a drawing. Give simple directions, focusing on lines, space, shape, dimensions, and position words. Examples: *Draw a triangle. Draw a long line over the top of the triangle. Be sure the line and the triangle touch. What did you draw? (see-saw) Draw a rectangle with a 4" top and bottom and 2" sides. On top of the rectangle, at the left corner, draw a 1"-high triangle. On top of the rectangle, at the right corner, draw a line up at an angle. Under the rectangle at the right and left corners, draw 1" circles. What did you draw? (baby carriage)*

***What Do You Think?***—Direct students to listen as you read them sentences and to mark on their answer sheets whether the sentences are true or false. Intersperse with correct sentences, sentences that are logically inconsistent. Examples: *The young lettuce asked for some milk. The student drove his book home to study.*

***Dictation***—Use the dictation format to practice sound/symbol associations, auditory discrimination, juncture sensitivity, and aural comprehension of words and sentences. For sounds and words: Tell students to listen as you say a sound and a word that begins with that sound, such as /p/ *pet* (listen to the word); then to listen a second time and write the spelling for the sound (word); then listen a third time to check their answers. For sentences and passages: Direct students to listen to the sentence or passage and to write it verbatim. You will read it three times: first, read the passage through at a moderate, conversational pace; next, read it slowly, breaking it into meaningful phrases of no more than five words each; finally, read the passage through at a moderate pace. Students should write the passage during the first two readings and check their work during the final reading.

***Getting the Facts***—Have students listen as you read a passage, then ask them questions about details in the passage. Answers can be multiple-choice, yes/no, or short statements.

***Information, Please***—Read a passage aloud to the class and have the students ask you questions about the action or information in the passage. As an alternative, students can write questions about the passage.

***News Report***—Select a narrative passage that describes an event. Direct students to listen and to fill in their answer sheets with the who, what, where, when, why, and how of the story.

*The ESL Teacher's Book of Lists,* © 1993 by John Wiley & Sons, Inc.

# 7-4  ACTIVITIES FOR DEVELOPING ORAL SKILLS

***Pretty Perfect Pronunciation***—Present a group of words with the target phoneme in the initial position and have students repeat the words after you. Read them clearly, but without exaggeration or distortion. Use of a rhythmic choral response will aid students' learning new sounds and allophones within words. Tape record the lists of words so that students can practice independently. Repeat the exercise with the phoneme presented in the final position, then in the medial position.

***A Big Pig***—Practice the pronunciation of problem phonemes using contrast pairs. Direct students to listen carefully and repeat after you as you read the pairs. Example: *b/p   bade/paid; bin/pin; big/pig; bet/pet.*

***Give Yourself a Hand***—Teach students to recognize differences in stress by having them clap out the rhythm of their English names. Use a loud clap for the accented or stressed syllable(s) and a soft clap for the unaccented or unstressed syllable(s). Examples: *MA-ry, Ma-RIE, ED-ward, THOM-as, JENN-i-fer, JOHN-ny.*

***Cadence Drills***—Give students lists of words having the same stress patterns. Model the correct stress pattern for sample words, then direct students to read them aloud in unison. Repeat the list reading until students develop a natural cadence for reading the various stress patterns. Use single-syllable words; two-syllable words with the accent on the first syllable; two-syllable words with the accent on the second syllable, and so forth.

***Sentence Tunes***—Have students read a series of similar sentences: statements, open questions, tag questions, yes/no questions, and so forth. Model the correct stress pattern with examples before the student response. Repeat the exercise to develop a natural cadence.

***Mother Goose and Company***—Use limericks, nursery rhymes, and short poems to teach and provide practice for American English intonation patterns. Recite them in choral groups and individually. Use proverbs and popular song lyrics for older students.

***Stressed Cloze***—Give students ten written sentences, each with a word deleted. Above the blank, show the stress pattern of the missing word. Use markings the students are familiar with from their texts, such as dots in descending size, or dashes and accent marks. Give three answer choices, each syntactically and semantically correct, but only one matching the stress pattern. Students choose the one that matches the pattern. Example: *Put the jar in the - - - - -. (cabinet) (refrigerator) (closet)*

***Charades***—Prepare a set of charades cards with active verb phrases. Ask a student to pick a card and act out the verb phrase. Have members of the class guess what the student is doing. Use a three-minute time limit per charade. Guesses should be stated in complete interrogative sentences, such as *Are you making a bed? Are you kneading dough?* This activity can be done as a team game with points for correct answers within the time allowed.

*Puppet Theater*—Using masks, puppets, and props students practice dialogues related to social and other situations.

*Role Life*—Teacher and student or student and student take on roles and play at various scenarios from everyday situations. For example, the teacher is the bank teller and the student wants to cash a check; the student is injured and asks a passerby (another student) for directions to a hospital or help in finding a doctor.

*Show and Tell*—Ask students to bring something into class and give a brief (three-minute) oral presentation about it. Suggest that students select items related to hobbies or culture. Preparation should include the learning of appropriate vocabulary and consideration of how to present new material to the class. Visual aids (charts, demonstrations, pantomimes, and so forth) may be helpful.

*Ms. Manners*—Have pairs of students pick a card at random from a set of concept cards that show people engaged in situations normally requiring standard dialogue. Students then act out the scenes in front of the class. Give students a few minutes to organize and rehearse. Use to review vocabulary, develop fluency, and practice social skills.

*Simon Says*—Use this children's game to review vocabulary, gestures, imperative structures, and many active verbs. Students follow Simon's directions as long as they are preceded by the statement "Simon says." Students can be selected to be Simon and directed to use words from a specific category, such as body parts, emotion words, or actions.

*Take a Hike*—Use this word game to develop fluency. The game requires students to chain nouns alphabetically. To begin say, *"I'm going to take a hike and I'm taking an (A word)."* The next person says, *"I'm going to take a hike and I'm taking a (B word),"* and so on, until a person is unable to think of an appropriate word in alphabetical sequence. To help keep things going while students' vocabularies are limited, supply a word when students cannot. The pace of the game should be brisk.

*Tie One On*—Use this word game to review and reinforce vocabulary in a specific category, such as food or sports. To begin, using the "food" category, student 1 says a food word (cake), then student 2 says another word from the category (hot dogs). Student 3 says another food word (cheese), and so on, until a student cannot think of a food word or makes a mistake. The next student begins the cycle again by announcing the new category and the first word. The game should be played at a fast pace.

*Tennis-Elbow-Foot*—This word game practices fluency and association. To begin, student 1 says a word, student 2 says a related word, student 3 says a word related to word 2, and so on, until the student next in turn cannot think of a related

*The ESL Teacher's Book of Lists,* © 1993 by John Wiley & Sons, Inc.

word or makes a mistake. The words in a cycle must be related, but do not have to be from the same category. For example: *knit, weave, basket, ball, bat, cave, mountain, Alps, Europe*. The game should be played briskly.

*Telephone Chain*—Use this children's game to encourage students to improve their pronunciation skills. To play, a message is whispered from one person to the next through a chain of ten persons. The tenth person repeats the message aloud. Teams can compete to see which one gets the message through with the least "interference."

*Take Two*—Divide the class into small groups. One person in each group is selected to be the director. The director "directs" groups of two to four students in acting out written skits using stage directions and directions for movement, gestures, tone, attitude, characterization, and so forth. The groups put on the skits for one another.

*Twenty Questions*—Select photographs or drawings of nouns in the students' vocabulary. A student picks one of the photographs without showing it to the class. Members of the class take turns asking questions about the item. Examples: *"Is it bigger than a book?" "Is there one in this room?" "Is it expensive?"* The student answers "yes" or "no." The questioning continues until someone can guess the item or until the class has reached twenty questions. This exercise develops fluency, vocabulary, grammar, and listening comprehension.

*Salesmanship*—Students select a product or service and "sell" it to the class. Students create poster ads, charts comparing "their" product with the "competition," and a sales pitch. Students make the sales presentations to the class.

*Headline News*—Divide the class into three-person reporting teams. One team each week (more often if your schedule permits) prepares a five- to seven-minute news feature on an approved topic. Focus on issues in independent living such as employment, banking, insurance, health issues, or social services. The team meets and works out an outline of the topic; team members decide on the distribution of research work; they research and write assigned parts; the members edit one another's work. The team presents its report orally. The use of graphs and other visual aids should be encouraged.

*Talk Show*—Students prepare background information on a given current-events topic. One student acts as the "talk show host" and leads a panel discussion and question-and-answer period. Four students are on a panel, and each gives a brief prepared presentation. The rest of the class participates in the question-and-answer session with the "audience." If possible, videotape the "show" and share with other classes. To prepare for the activity, show the class a taped TV talk show and focus students' attention on format, personal interactions, and vocabulary used.

*Ask Me Again*—Do a rapid oral drill, asking each student a different question but using the same structure. For each question type, give one or two model questions and answers before asking students to respond. Ask questions that have these types of responses: yes or no; yes or no with a restatement; yes or no with a counterstatement; yes or no with a partial statement; yes or no with a synonymous statement; a short answer (one word or phrase); or a complete sentence.

***Backing up***—Practice intonation patterns by using a backward build-up drill. In backward build-up, you begin with the last word, then in each repetition you add the preceding word. Students repeat after each addition. This method maintains the correct intonation pattern throughout the multiple repetitions.

> EXAMPLE:   *"John got an A on the test today."*
> *"today."* (students repeat)
> *"test today."* (repeat)
> *"on the test today."* (repeat)
> *"an A on the test today."* (repeat)
> *"got an A on the test today."* (repeat)
> *"John got an A on the test today."* (repeat)

***Changing Your Tune***—Divide the class into groups of three and present a situation. The first group role plays the situation as originally stated. For the second group, change the context and have them alter their register, manner, and so forth, while preserving the storyline. Change the context for each group.

> FOR EXAMPLE:   *asking one's brother for a loan; asking a banker for a loan; asking one's father for a loan; asking a stranger on the street for a loan.*

***TV Times***—Send for the transcript of one of the class's favorite television sitcoms and rehearse the lines of the show with a cast selected from the class. Present a "reading" of the show to the class.

***Exhausting Your Options***—This exercise should be done as a game. Have all students stand. Then begin by asking the first student a question, such as *Where did you go yesterday?* After the student answers, repeat the question for the next student, and so on, continuing until a student cannot respond with a new answer and sits back down. Then change the question and continue to play until only one student remains and is declared the winner.

***Between the Lines***—Have students listen to a taped dialogue. Ask students questions that go beyond the literal meaning of the conversation.

> EXAMPLES:   *Why did Mary react the way she did when Tom told her what happened? How do you think Mary felt? What was Tom trying to do? Did Tom do the right thing? How would you have handled the problem?*

***Career Plans***—Have students tell the class, one at a time, what they want to do on their first (or next) job. They should identify the type of work, something about what it entails, and why they want to do it. They should also tell what skills are needed to do the job and how they plan to prepare for it if they don't already have the skills.

*The ESL Teacher's Book of Lists,* © 1993 by John Wiley & Sons, Inc.

# 7-5 ACTIVITIES FOR VOCABULARY DEVELOPMENT

*Introducing . . .* —Introduce vocabulary by presenting the object and the spoken word together. Use the actual object, pantomimes, demonstrations, gestures, series pictures, photographs, or other means to show the meaning of the target word. After saying the word three times, ask students to repeat it after you. Then use the word in a sentence or a meaningful phrase. Choral repetition should precede individual response.

*Not So Basic*—When introducing basic vocabulary, show students several examples of the target concept. For example: if the target word is "dog," show several different sizes, colors, and breeds of dogs. This eliminates inappropriate associations. After students learn the target word, review the examples, adding the word for the differentiating characteristic.

FOR EXAMPLE: *a black dog, a tan dog, a black-and-white dog, a small dog, a large dog.*

*All Sorts*—Select twenty vocabulary words from a single lexical group and four appropriate descriptive categories. Create a chart using the categories for column headings and the vocabulary words for the rows. Direct students to put an X in each category that describes the vocabulary words. Example:

| **Vocabulary** | **Categories** | | | |
|---|---|---|---|---|
| | *male* | *female* | *old* | *young* |
| father | x | | x | |
| girl | | x | | x |
| child | | | | x |
| grandmother | | x | x | |

*Word Maps*—Introduce sets of related vocabulary, defining each word as you present it. Engage students in a discussion of the relationships among the words and create semantic maps by writing the words on the chalkboard and showing, by placement and connecting lines, the relationships among the concepts presented. Common descriptors, such as category names, may be added to the map for detail.

*Mix-up*—Give students several pairs of mixed-up sentences and have them repair and rewrite them. The errors should be lexical.

EXAMPLES: *I was so hungry I went to sleep. I was so tired I had dinner.*

*Cognate Review*—Give students lists of words that are cognates in English and in their native language. Select cognate concepts and terms that are already understood by students in their native language. Read the English word of the pair and have the students repeat it after you. Help students recognize spelling conversion patterns such as: *tion/cion* and *ly/mente.*

*Content Cognates*—Prepare a grammar review or other structure-centered class around a content subject and use cognates to make the lesson a more natural presentation of language in context. The use of cognates results in a more mature level of language than what usually occurs with the limited high-frequency vocabulary from prepared lessons, particularly in the early stages of language learning. This activity will help students make the transition to English-only content area instruction.

*Want Ads*—Teach job-related vocabulary by presenting job titles with job descriptions and lists of qualifications as they would appear in a newspaper advertisement.

> EXAMPLE: *Wanted: Auto mechanic to tune engines, change oil, change filters, and fix flat tires. Must know how to use a jack, socket wrench, gauges, and other tools.*

*Crossword Puzzles*—Have students complete crossword puzzles as a review of the definitions and spelling of new vocabulary words. Weekly crosswords can be habit forming and a painless way to continue to review vocabulary and spelling.

*Descriptors*—Have students cut out several newspaper and magazine ads for target items, such as vacations, banks, stereo equipment, cars. Students make a chart and, for each item, list the adjectives or other descriptive language used. Discuss the similarity and appeal of descriptors for each item. This activity helps students with connotation and with categorizing words (scientific, glamorous, safety, light-hearted).

*Synonyms/Antonyms*—Give students a list of word pairs and have them indicate whether they are synonyms or antonyms. An alternative activity is to present two columns of words: in column A, the target words, in column B, the synonyms or antonyms. Students match the two columns.

*Word-Search Puzzles*—Have students do word-search puzzles that contain the target vocabulary words for a current lesson or words from prior vocabulary lessons. This activity helps reinforce students' visual memory of the words as well as their spellings.

*Survey*—Develop a survey of students' hobbies and extracurricular activities. For each item have students indicate how often they participate: always, often, sometimes, rarely, never. Have students tabulate the results. Distribute results and direct individual students to report on the participation rate for a particular hobby or activity.

> EXAMPLES: *Five out of eight people watch TV often, two out of eight people watch TV sometimes, and one out of eight never watches TV.*

*Subject Pictionaries*—Create a specialized "pictionary" for a content subject by mounting titled drawings or pictures on 3″ × 5″ or 5″ × 8″ prepunched index cards and arranging them alphabetically in a card binder. Students use the pictionaries to learn the vocabulary and to look up a word and its spelling.

*Really?*—Give students a list of sentences, many having embedded lexical errors, and direct them to indicate whether the sentence is "true" or "false."

EXAMPLES: *The cat studied for a geometry test.*    *T/F*
*The fisherman caught a tuna.*    *T/F*
*The sunny weather was annoying.*    *T/F*

*Flash*—Pair students, an advanced student with a beginner, for word-recognition flashcard drills. The advanced student shows the beginner the picture of the object and says the word; the beginner repeats. Flashcards with the written form of the word can be used for word-recognition drills if the concept is already known. The pace should be brisk. As an alternative, students at the same level of skill can be paired and can take turns drilling each other. When both students are stumped by a word, they should put the card aside for teacher assistance.

*Mirror, Mirror*—Pantomime new vocabulary words and say them. Have students mirror your actions and repeat the words. After you have introduced and repeated a few words and feel the students are fairly comfortable with them, speed up the pantomimes and repeat them in random order.

*Object/Article Card Drills*—Review vocabulary and appropriate articles using concept cards. Deal a set of concept cards face down to all players. Begin by turning over the top card on your pile (a cat) and saying, "I have a cat." The student to the right then turns over his or her card (object) and says, "I have a (object)." Students continue in turn until all cards have been used. Correct for articles and partitives. Points can be added to a score for correct responses and subtracted for errors.

*Charades*—To review vocabulary, students pick a card with the vocabulary word written on it and gesture, pantomime, or otherwise dramatize the word. Members of the class guess the word. This is a good team game.

*Mix and Match*—Teach basic Latin and Greek prefixes, suffixes, and root words. On a worksheet, students match words based on these elements in column A with the definitions provided in column B.

*Content Quick*—Begin as early as possible to introduce groups of related content subject vocabulary in regular drills. Use pictures, concept cards, and so forth. Example at the word level: *map, ocean, Christopher Columbus, ships, Indians, America.* At the sentence level:

*Christopher Columbus had a map.*
*Christopher Columbus had three ships.*
*Christopher Columbus saw the ocean.*
*Christopher Columbus saw the Indians.*
*Christopher Columbus saw America.*

Use of content words throughout the language learning experience helps students make the transition to appropriate grade level content subject texts.

***Close in the Vocabulary Gaps***—Have students practice recognizing and spelling new vocabulary words by completing cloze passages. In the beginning, give students the list of vocabulary words for the exercise to ensure correct spelling.

***Clued in***—Give students a list of related words that have connotative information for an event or circumstance and direct the students to group the words that "go together" best. Examples for store and school scenarios: *cashier, desk, chalk, hangers, dressing room, dictionary.* Examples for two restaurant scenarios: *waitress, musicians, chef, coat hook, tablecloths, plastic-covered menu, candles, paper napkins, a counter, a take-out sign.*

***Close Relatives***—Develop a chart on the chalkboard or overhead showing the adjective/noun/adverb/verb forms of the same root word. Help students form generalizations about the forms. Example:

| | | | |
|---|---|---|---|
| *sad* | *sadness* | *sadly* | *to sadden* |
| *happy* | *happiness* | *happily* | *to be happy* |
| *sick* | *sickness* | *sickly* | *to sicken* |

***Very Punny***—Use puns or jokes to help students learn multiple meanings and connotations of words. There are many pun books available commercially. Humor should be a regular part of the instructional plan. It makes classwork fun, and it motivates students to attend carefully to word meaning.

***Shades of Meaning***—Give students lists of words dealing with the same trait, characteristic, and so forth, and help them arrange the words on a continuum from least to most.

EXAMPLES: *smirk, chuckle, giggle, laugh, belly laugh*
*mist, drizzle, rain, downpour, deluge*

***Facts in Five***—Make a five-by-five grid, a set of category cards (animals, parts of the body, places, school subjects, people, and so forth) and a set of alphabet letters (not including Q, U, X, Y, or Z). Ask a student to pick five category cards and read them to the class. Students write the category names across the five spaces of the grid. Ask another student to select five alphabet cards and read them aloud. Students write the letters along the five blocks at the left of the grid. Allow the class three to five minutes to fill in the grid with appropriate words. Example: if one of the categories was animals and the letters were B, M, L, C, G, the column under the heading animal might be filled in with the words *bear, mouse, lion, cat, giraffe.*

***'Tis the Season***—Pick a season; have students compete to see who can write down the most words that have some relationship to the season. They must be able to state a relationship if challenged.

EXAMPLE: *Spring: rain, crocuses, baseball, jelly beans, mud, buds, warm, sweaters,* and so forth. As an alternative, give the students a list of fifty words and the season and have them circle the words that relate to the season.

*The ESL Teacher's Book of Lists,* © 1993 by John Wiley & Sons, Inc.

# 7–6  *ACTIVITIES FOR GRAMMAR INSTRUCTION*

*Sentence Flips*—Select two sets of concept cards: nouns and active verbs. Place the two sets face up and side by side. Ask students to look at the noun/verb pair and, in a complete sentence, tell what the two cards show. Go through the card sets using three substitution patterns: first, flip through the verb set and create sentences with the first noun and each of the verbs, then the second noun and each of the verbs, and so forth; second, reverse the pattern and flip through the noun set; third, flip the cards from both sets, creating a new sentence each time. Use singular and plural nouns to give practice for number agreement.

*Markers*—Present noun phrases that show the correct use of a/an and explain the rule. Present one of the noun phrases in a model sentence and direct students to replace the target word ( ) with the new cued word ( ). This can be done as a written or oral exercise.

> EXAMPLE: *I bought a (book) on Tuesday.*
> *(vase) (orange) (purse) (umbrella).*

*Yes It Is/No It's Not*—Present model pairs of positive and negative statements.

> FOR EXAMPLE: *It is snowing.  It is not snowing.*
> *It is raining.  It is not raining.*

Then, read a positive sentence (*It is foggy.*) and ask students to respond with its negative form (*It is not foggy.*). Responses may be made by the whole class or by individual students. Repeat the exercise, using alternate forms of the negative:

> *It is raining.  It isn't raining.*
> *It is raining.  It's not raining.*

Repeat the exercise, presenting the negative form and having students respond with the positive. Example: *She doesn't have a pen. She has a pen.*

*Question*—Present model pairs of a statement and its question form.

> FOR EXAMPLE: *It is snowing.  Is it snowing?*
> *It is raining.  Is it raining?*

Then read a statement and have students give the question form. Responses can be made by the whole class or by individuals.

*Time Lapse Pictures*—Show students sets of three related pictures depicting an action about to happen, in progress, and that has obviously occurred. Describe the pictures as you show them. For example, if the first picture in the set shows a boy on a diving board about to dive into a pool, say *"The boy will dive into the pool."* For the second picture with the boy in the air, say, *"The boy is diving into the pool."* For the last picture, showing the boy descending into the depths of the pool, say, *"The boy dove into the pool."* After presenting an example, have students supply the sentences as you show them sets of actions in time sequence.

*Timeline*—Create a timeline marked in hours, days, or years and show when several events occurred. Include a mark for the present time and marks for events that will occur in the future. Ask students questions about the relative time of the events and direct them to respond in complete sentences. Examples based on a timeline of John's day: *Did John leave home before or after breakfast? John left after breakfast. When will John meet Jim? John will meet Jim after school.*

*Learning One's Place*—Using word cards and a pocket board, arrange the cards to show proper sentence word order, including the placement of adjectives and adverbs, negatives, and question words. Have students practice the structures by replacing word cards to make new sentences in proper order.

*Condensed Thoughts*—Give students a pair of sentences and have them condense the ideas of both into one, taking care to make all correlative changes for number, subject-verb agreement, and so forth. Examples:

*Are they in the library? Are they studying?*
*Are they studying in the library?*
*The dress is too big. Jean cannot wear it.*
*The dress is too big for Jean to wear.*

*Meaningful Mates*—Give students two columns of basic sentences and a list of conjunctions. Have students make as many meaningful sentences as possible by joining a sentence from column A with one from column B using the contractions.

*Compare and Contrast*—Present two items that share some characteristics, such as a chair and a table. Have students write statements using "and" or "but" to compare and contrast the items. Examples:

*The chair has a seat, but the table has a top.*
*The chair has a back, but the table has no back.*
*The chair has four legs, and the table has four legs.*

*Sub Drill*—Give students sentences with proper or common nouns and direct them to replace the nouns with pronouns. In the beginning of the drill, cue the response; later, do not cue the response. Examples:

*Billy has the notebook. (he) He has the notebook. (it) He has it.*
*The teacher has the book. She has the book. She has it.*

*Keeping It Straight*—Select a passage of 200 to 250 words that includes pronouns and other anaphora. Direct students to circle all the words that refer to the same person or thing. Example: **John Wills** *was on a new job. The **detective** always had interesting work to do. When **he** met **his** client at the office something told **John** it would be more interesting than usual.*

*Reflexives*—Present the reflexive pronouns in pairs with the personal pronouns: *I - myself; you - yourself,* and so forth. Have students repeat each pair. Present a model sentence: *"I painted the desk by myself,"* then a cue, *"she."* Direct students to make the replacements needed by the cue: *She painted the desk by herself.* Continue with each reflexive pronoun and several model sentences.

*More or Less*—Present a graph or pictograph comparing six things, such as the numbers of people who like six different candies. Ask students questions, using the vocabulary for inequalities, equalities, and comparisons. Examples: *Which candy is liked by the most people? The least? Which candies were liked more than X? Which candy was liked more than X but less than Y?*

*Do You Agree?*—Have students select a topic and conduct an opinion survey on the issue, then help them create simple graphs or pie charts comparing responses. Have students write a report of the results, using the vocabulary for inequalities, equalities, and comparisons.

*Wishful Thinking*—Provide practice for the conditional tense by having students complete the sentences:

*If I had an X . . .*
*If I were to win the lottery . . .*
*If I had only known . . .*
*If I hadn't seen the car . . .*
*If I hadn't been late . . .*

*When I Was a Child . . .* —Have students write their autobiographies, paying careful attention to the proper use of past tenses, sequence, and transition words.

*Crystal Ball*—Ask students to "look into the crystal ball" and to write about the lives they will have in the next five years. Direct their attention to the use of the future tense, sequence, cause and effect, and transition words.

*It's the Law*—Direct students to compose a set of rules for one of the following: the kitchen, the classroom, good citizenship, being a good neighbor, or being a good friend. Attention should be given to imperative structures and modals.

*Gotcha*—Prepare a text of 200 to 250 words by embedding errors of one grammatical type, such as improper pronoun use or tense shifts. Have students read the text, then have them edit it to correct the errors. Tell students the number, but not type of errors that are in the passage.

*Ripple Effects*—Use a moving slot substitution to practice correlative changes required by a replacement word. Present a sentence and cue the word that will be used as the substitute. Vary the slot in the sentence for the substitution. Example: *Carol has a white cat. (dog) Carol has a white dog. (we) We have a white dog. (brown) We have a brown dog. (two) We have two brown dogs.*

*Expansion*—Present a basic sentence and cue students to make additions. Students repeat the complete expanded sentence after each cue. Example: *The girl swims. (young) The young girl swims. (gracefully) The young girl swims gracefully. (in the pool) The young girl swims gracefully in the pool.*

*Hangman*—The children's game of hangman can be used to review spelling. Students should work in pairs and compete. The computer version of hangman is effective for intermediate and older students.

# 7-7 ACTIVITIES FOR IMPROVING WRITING SKILLS

*Pen Pals*—Have students write letters to one another without knowing their "pen pal's" identity. Randomly assign each student a number, then have students draw numbers out of a hat to pick a pen pal. Suggest that first letters be autobiographical and include information about the students' hobbies and other activities.

*May I?*—Collect the addresses of government agencies, businesses, and other groups that offer free informative booklets or samples. Several catalogues of such addresses, including those for curriculum-related giveaways, are available. Have students write letters asking for an item they would like to receive. Stress letter format and address components.

*Class News*—Help students launch a class newspaper. Include standard news features dealing with current events, a school events feature, a cultural feature, study advice, and the like. In the beginning it may be necessary to provide substantial support for the newspaper, but as students' skills develop they can take on assignments, editing, format, and so forth.

*Favorite People*—Have students write fan letters to their favorite television or movie stars or athletes. In the letters, students may express their opinions, compliment the individual, ask for a photograph, and so on.

*Picture This Competition*—Give students a basic two-word sentence such as, "Boys play." Students then add modifiers to the basic sentence, including adjectives, adverbs, adjectival and adverbial phrases. Students can compete individually or in small groups to see who can create the greatest number of different sentences in ten minutes. Examples: *Boys play. The older boys play tubas. The tall boys play basketball. The young boys play with blocks.*

*News Flash*—To keep students abreast of the news, have students write a news flash when a special or unusual event occurs. A news flash is similar to a language experience chart. The students contribute information and dictate the story. The teacher writes the story out on newsprint or, if possible, types it into a word processor. Copies are made and distributed. When it is completed, read each sentence to the group and have them repeat the reading as you point to the words. After two or more repetitions, distribute individual copies of the news flash. This activity introduces topical vocabulary in high-interest areas and helps to link students to important events around them.

*No Telegraph Today*—Give students several pages from a major newspaper and ask them to rewrite the headlines into complete, correct sentences.

*You're in the Headlines*—Have students write headlines for ten important events in their own lives.

*House Party*—Have students write directions from school to their homes or to their favorite restaurants or parks. Attention should be given to direction vocabulary, sequence, and proper names (streets, place names).

*Gist*—After students have practiced an oral dialogue, have them write a paragraph that tells the gist of the dialogue.

*What's Going On?*—Give students concept cards that depict people engaged in activities or situations. Ask students to write as much about the picture as they can.

*Travel Agent*—Provide timetables for bus, train, and taxi, and a chart of the time it takes to travel between destinations by each mode of transportation. Have students plan an itinerary for a trip from one city to another. Give conditions, such as: *can't leave before 8* A.M. *or arrive after midnight; shouldn't have more than one hour stopover in any single place.* Students should work in pairs to practice travel vocabulary. The itinerary should be written out in a specified format. Attention should be given to abbreviations, logical connections, sequence, proper nouns, and punctuation.

*Reporter*—Have students conduct oral interviews, take notes, and write an article on the person they interviewed. Students should not report on the person who interviewed them.

*Graduation Party*—Working in small groups, have students write a proposal for a graduation party. The students decide on a "theme" for decorations, a price per person, the type of site, the dinner menu, and the type of entertainment. Provide a "How to plan a party" brochure from a caterer, a phone book, travel and dining books, and newspaper ads for caterers and restaurants. Students prepare a proposal with options, giving a brief narrative description of the affair and suitable sites, with names, addresses, costs per person, benefits, and so forth. The research for the proposal is done using the materials supplied; however, advanced classes may be required to also make one or two phone calls for price-per-person estimates. The proposals should follow a specified format. Give a worksheet or short sample.

*There Ought to Be a Law*—Have students write essays on a pet peeve or on a matter of serious concern. The essay should focus on problem/solutions or cause/effect. Topics might include: alternative energy sources, pollution of the oceans and rivers, seatbelts on school buses, drug sales, street crime, homelessness, and unemployment.

*Outlines*—Select well-constructed passages of 200 to 250 words from a content subject text at an appropriate reading level. Give students copies. Working with the whole group, teach students to select the key ideas for an outline by crossing out information that is not important or by underlining or highlighting the important information. Once students can identify the key ideas, they can develop the outline with minimal assistance.

*Scenes from a School*—Distribute photographs of activities that take place at school. The scenes should cover the ordinary (cafeteria lines) and the special (graduation). Students select a picture and write a story about the event.

*Advice Column*—Each student writes a letter to "Dear Gabby" for advice and signs the letter with a pseudonym. After the letters are put in a box, each student picks one out and answers it. The answers are put back in the box and then distributed

*The ESL Teacher's Book of Lists*, © 1993 by John Wiley & Sons, Inc.

in a "mail call." Students read the replies aloud. This can be done as a humorous exercise or with some seriousness.

***Diamante***—Have students write diamantes, or diamond-shaped poems. In this poetic form, the writer goes from one idea to its opposite in an organized way. The first line is a noun. Line 2 has two adjectives that describe the noun. Line 3 has three verbs that end in -ing and are related to the noun. Line 4 is the transition line. It has four nouns. The first two relate to the original noun. The second two relate to an opposite noun that will be named in line 7. Line 5 has three -ing verbs related to the noun in line 7. Line 6 has two adjectives related to line 7. And line 7 is the noun that is opposite line 1. Example:

> *Summer*
> *hot, sunny*
> *swimming, playing, sailing*
> *picnics, vacation; school, holidays*
> *sledding, skiing, studying*
> *cold, snowy*
> *Winter*

***What Characters!***—Distribute cartoons or several frames of a comic strip that have empty dialogue balloons. Have students write in the dialogue or captions. Note: There are several commercially available sets that are great fun.

***One-Two-Three***—Give students sets of directions for common activities, such as making a sandwich or washing dishes. The directions should be out of order and mixed up. For example, one direction in making the sandwich might be to spread mayonnaise on the lid instead of on the bread. Give no more than eight steps for each activity. Students rewrite the directions in proper order and with logical connections. Note: The mix-ups add interest to the activity and require students to do more than simply recopy sentences. Fixing the inconsistencies will require making correlative changes.

***Stolen Property***—Have students fill in an insurance form for a claim based on a hypothetical break-in to their homes. Attention should be given to the special terms of the report, the narrative about the incident, and the need for accuracy.

***Fender Bender***—Have students fill in a police report about a hypothetical car accident. Give attention to special vocabulary, the narrative about the accident (sequence, cause/effect, who did what, and so forth), and the need for accuracy.

# 7-8  SELECTED INSTRUCTIONAL MATERIALS

## AUDITORY/AURAL SKILLS

*Advanced Listening Comprehension*—P. Dunekl and F. Pialorsi (Newbury House); cassettes of mini-lectures for advanced practice in listening comprehension and notetaking.

*Listening Tasks for Intermediate Students of American English*—S. Schecter (Cambridge University Press); cassette/workbook format for listen-and-do exercises.

*Now Hear This!*—B. Foley (Newbury House); cassettes of conversations, descriptions, and narratives to develop listening comprehension.

## GRAMMAR SKILLS

*GrammarWork*—P. Breyer (Prentice Hall Regents); grammar practice in context exercises.

*Regents English Workbooks*—R. Dixson (Prentice Hall Regents); comprehensive, sequential grammar instruction and practice.

*Structure Practice in Context*—P. Laporte and J. Maurer (Longman); grammar workbook using context-based exercises and focusing on individual grammar items.

*Visions*—E. Lites and J. Lehman (Prentice Hall Regents); grammar instruction and practice in communicative context.

*Writing and Combining Standard English Sentences*—A. Pack and L. Henrichsen (Newbury House); basic sentence construction, transformations, and combining techniques.

*The ESL Teacher's Book of Lists*, © 1993 by John Wiley & Sons, Inc.

## ORAL SKILLS

*Can't Stop Talking*—G. Rooks (Newbury House); problem-solving situations and structured activities for building conversation skills.

*Clear Speech*—J. Gilbert (Cambridge University Press); practice for pronunciation, stress, and intonation patterns in context.

*Comics and Conversation*—J. Ashkenas (Pro Lingua Associates); uncaptioned cartoon stories.

*Conversation Inspirations for ESL*—N. Zelman (Pro Lingua Associates); suggestions for interviews, talks, role plays, problem solving, chain stories, and discussions.

*Images Conversation Cards*—G. Zuern (Addison-Wesley); uses oversized photograph flashcards as conversation cues.

*Jass Chants*—Carolyn Graham (Oxford University Press); chants and poems for stress and intonation instruction.

*Listen for It*—J. Richards, D. Gordon, and A. Harper (Oxford University Press); cassette/workbook listening comprehension skills.

*On Speaking Terms*—J. Harris, R. Hube, and S. Vogel (Maxwell Macmillan); 102 short dialogues with activities, cassette.

*Person to Person*—J. Richards and D. Bycina (Oxford University Press); situational conversation practice for fluency.

*Phrase by Phrase*—M. Chan (Prentice Hall Regents); text/cassette program for practice in pronunciation, stress, intonation, sound production, and listening.

*Picture Stories for Beginning Communication*—S. Heyer (Prentice Hall Regents); humor-based conversation practice with target grammar structures.

*Pronouncing American English*—G. Orion (Newbury House); cassettes/activities to develop pronunciation, stress, and intonation.

*Skits in English*—M. Hines (Prentice Hall Regents); scripts and role playing in common situations.

## VOCABULARY SKILLS

*101 American English Idiom Learning Cards*—Harry Collis (National Textbook Company); flashcards with context passages or dialogues.

*A Vocabulary Workbook: Prefixes, Roots and Suffixes for ESL Students*—A. Farid (Prentice Hall Regents); teaches the meaning of common word roots and affixes and how to use them to discover the meaning of unfamiliar words.

*Advanced English Vocabulary*—H. Barnard (Newbury House); workbook exercises and dictation to develop knowledge of 2,000 words commonly used in lectures, newspapers, and texts.

*Advanced Vocabulary Games*—L. Schinke-Llano (National Textbook Company); duplicating masters for word games to practice and master high-frequency vocabulary and useful expressions.

*Easy English Learning Cards*—(Flame Co.); 120 flashcards of basic vocabulary.

*Essential Idioms in English*—R. Dixson (Prentice Hall Regents); classic texts for practice with 500 of the most common English idioms.

*Survival Vocabulary Flashcard Books and Workbooks*—J. Richey (Janus Books); presents 80 words per independent-living topic with games and activities.

*Take It Easy: American Idioms*—P. McPartland (Prentice Hall Regents); contextual presentation and practice for 164 verb idioms.

*The New Oxford Picture Dictionary*—E. C. Parnwell (Oxford University Press); 2,400 words presented in context illustrations.

*Vocabulary Playing Cards*—(Oxford University Press); 40 cards contextually illustrating everyday vocabulary.

## WRITING SKILLS

*Effective Writing*—J. Withrow (Cambridge University Press); composition exercises for intermediate-level students leading to competent essay writing.

*Focus on Composition*—A. Raimes (Oxford University Press); visual stimuli and model passages that develop good writing.

*From Writing to Composing*—B. Ingram and C. King (Cambridge University Press); composition exercises for beginning- to intermediate-level ESL students.

*Start Writing*—F. Bacheller (Prentice Hall Regents); develops basic writing skills and mechanics of structure, punctuation, spelling, and capitalization.

*Write Soon!*—E. Prince (Maxwell Macmillan); progressive exercises from simple sentences to full-length essays.

*Written English*—R. Rainsbury (Prentice Hall Regents); workbook for extensive practice in writing mechanics.

*The ESL Teacher's Book of Lists,* © 1993 by John Wiley & Sons, Inc.

# 7-9 PUBLISHERS OF ESL CURRICULUM MATERIALS

**Addison-Wesley Publishing Company**
2725 Sand Hill Road
Menlo Park, CA 94025
1-800-447-2226
(Elementary/Intermediate/Secondary/
  Adult: ESL/Bilingual)

**AISI, Inc.**
9553 Valparaiso Court
Indianapolis, IN 46268
1-317-875-4085
(Elementary/Special Ed./Language
  Development: Language Software)

**Alemany Press**
A Division of Janus Book Publishers, Inc.
2501 Industrial Parkway West
Hayward, CA 94545
1-800-227-2375
(Elementary/Intermediate/Secondary/
  Adult: ESL, Bilingual)

**Ballard & Tighe Publishers**
480 Atlas Street
Brea, CA 92621
1-800-321-IDEA
(Elementary/Intermediate/Secondary/
  Adult: ESL/Bilingual/Language
  Software)

**Book-Lab**
P.O. Box 7316
500 74th Street
North Bergen, NJ 07047
1-201-861-6763
(Elementary/Intermediate/Secondary/
  Adult: ESL, Bilingual)

**Cambridge University Press**
40 West 20th Street
New York, NY 10011
1-800-227-0247
(Secondary/Adult: ESL)

**Center for Applied Research in
  Education**
P.O. Box 11071

Des Moines, IA 50336
1-800-288-4745
(Elementary/Intermediate/Secondary:
  ESL)

**Contemporary Books, Inc.**
180 North Michigan Avenue
Chicago, IL 60601
1-800-621-1918
(Intermediate/ Secondary/Adult: ESL)

**Crane Publishing Company**
1301 Hamilton Avenue
P.O. Box 3713
Trenton, NJ 08629
1-800-533-6279
(Elementary/Intermediate/Secondary:
  Language Software)

**Delta Systems Co., Inc.**
570 Rock Road Drive
Dundee, IL 60118
1-800-323-8270
(Elementary/Intermediate/Secondary/
  Adult: ESL, Bilingual)

**DLM**
P.O. Box 4000
One DLM Park
Allen, TX 75002
1-800-527-4747
(Elementary/Intermediate:
  ESL/Language Software)

**E.S.P., Inc.**
Teachers Center—Department B
P.O. Box 727
138 North Street
Middletown, NY 10940
1-914-342-5953
(Intermediate/Secondary/Adult:
  Language, ESL)

**Educational Activities, Inc.**
P.O. Box 392
Freeport, NY 11520
1-800-645-3739

(Elementary/Intermediate/Secondary/
  Adult: ESL/Bilingual)

**Flame Company**
1476 Pleasantville Road
Briarcliff Manor, NY 10510
1-800-535-2632
(Elementary/Intermediate/Secondary/
  Adult/Special Ed.: ESL/Bilingual/
  Language Software)

**Frank Schaffer Publications**
Teachers Center—Department 90
P.O. Box 727
138 North Street
Middletown, NY 10940
1-914-342-5953
(Elementary/Intermediate/Secondary:
  ESL, Language Development)

**Franklin Learning Resources,
  Education Division of Franklin
  Computer**
122 Burrs Road
Mt. Holly, NJ 08060
1-800-525-9673
(Elementary/Intermediate/Secondary/
  Adult: Language Software)

**Good Apple**
Teachers Center—Department B
P.O. Box 727
138 North Street
Middletown, NY 10940
1-914-342-5953
(Elementary/Intermediate/Secondary:
  ESL, Language Development)

**Hampton-Brown Books for Bilingual
  Education**
P.O. Box 223220
Carmel, CA 93922
1-800-333-3510
(Elementary: Bilingual)

**Heinle & Heinle**
20 Park Plaza
Boston, MA 02116
1-800-237-0053
(Intermediate/Secondary/Adult: ESL)

**Janus Book Publishers, Inc.**
2501 Industrial Parkway West
Department KJ
Hayward, CA 94545
1-800-227-2375
(Secondary/Special Ed.: ESL)

**Lectorum Publications, Inc.**
137 West 14th Street
New York, NY 10011
1-800-345-5946
(Elementary/Intermediate: Bilingual)

**Linmore Publishing**
P.O. Box 1545
Palatine, IL 60078
1-815-223-7499
(Secondary/Adult: ESL)

**Longman Inc.**
95 Church Street
White Plains, NY 10601
1-800-447-2226
(Intermediate/Secondary/Adult: ESL)

**Maxwell Macmillan International
  Publishing Group**
ESL/EFL Department
866 Third Avenue
New York, NY 10022
1-212-490-2600
(Secondary/Adult: ESL)

**Macmillan/McGraw-Hill Publishing
  Co.**
Front and Brown Streets
Riverside, NJ 08075-1197
1-609-461-2205
(Elementary/Intermediate: ESL,
  Spanish, Transition)

**McGraw-Hill College Division**
P.O. Box 456
Hightstown, NJ 08520
1-800-McGRAW-H ext. ESL
(Secondary/Adult: ESL)

**Milliken Publishing Company**
1100 Research Boulevard
St. Louis, MO 63132
1-800-333-READ

(Elementary/Intermediate/Secondary:
  ESL, Language Development)

**Minerva Books, Ltd.**
137 West 14th Street
New York, NY 10011
1-212-929-2852
(Intermediate/Secondary/Adult: ESL)

**National Textbook Company**
4255 West Touhy Avenue
Lincolnwood, IL 60646
1-800-323-4900
(Elementary/Intermediate/Secondary/
  Adult: ESL/Bilingual)

**Newbury House Publishers,**
  **A Division of Harper & Row**
10 East 53rd Street
New York, NY 10022
1-800-233-4190
(Secondary/Adult: ESL)

**New Readers Press, Division of**
  **Laubach Literacy International**
Department 92
Box 131
Syracuse, NY 13210
1-800-448-8878
(Intermediate/Secondary/Adult: Basic
  Literacy and ESL)

**Oxford University Press**
16-00 Pollitt Drive
Fair Lawn, NJ 07410
1-800-451-7556
(Elementary/Intermediate/Secondary/
  Adult: ESL)

**Prentice Hall Regents**
200 Old Tappan Road
Old Tappan, NJ 07675
1-800-223-1360
(Elementary/Intermediate/Secondary/
  Adult: ESL, Bilingual)

**Pro Lingua Associates**
15 Elm Street
Brattleboro, VT 05301
1-800-366-4775
(Intermediate/Secondary/Adult: ESL)

**QUERCUS**
Simon & Schuster School Group
4350 Equity Drive
P.O. Box 2649
Columbus, OH 43216
1-800-848-9500
(Secondary/Adult/Special Ed.: ESL)

**Scholastic Inc.**
P.O. Box 7502
Jefferson City, MO 65102
1-800-325-6149
(Elementary/Intermediate/Secondary:
  ESL/Language Software)

**Scott, Foresman and Company**
1900 East Lake Avenue
Glenview, IL 60025
1-800-554-4411
(Elementary/Intermediate/Secondary:
  ESL/Bilingual)

**Steck-Vaughn Company**
P.O. Box 26015
Austin, TX 78755
1-800-531-5015
(Secondary/Adult: ESL)

**University of Michigan Press**
839 Greene Street
P.O. Box 1104
Ann Arbor, MI 48106
1-313-764-4392
(Intermediate/Secondary/Adult: ESL)

**University of Pittsburgh Press,**
  **c/o CUP Services**
Box 6525
Ithaca, NY 14850
1-800-666-2211
(Intermediate/Secondary/Adult: ESL)

**Walker and Company**
Box 14
720 Fifth Avenue
New York, NY 10019
1-800-AT-WALKER
(Elementary/Secondary: Language,
  Reading)

# 7-10 ASSOCIATIONS AND RESOURCE CENTERS FOR ESL TEACHERS

**American Association of Applied Linguistics (AAAL)**
1325 18th Street, NW, Suite 211
Washington, D.C. 20036
202-835-1714

**American Council of Teachers of Foreign Languages (ACTFL)**
6 Executive Plaza
Yonkers, NY 10701-6801
914-963-8830

**American Dialect Society**
Department of English
MacMurry College
Jacksonville, IL 62650
217-245-6151

**Center for Applied Linguistics (CAL)**
1118 22nd Street, NW
Washington, D.C. 20037
202-467-0867

**Chapter 1 Technical Assistance Center**
Advanced Technology, Inc.
2601 Fortune Circle East, Suite 300A
Indianapolis, IN 46241
800-456-2380

**Council for Exceptional Children Division for Culturally and Linguistically Diverse Exceptional Learners (DDEL)**
1920 Association Drive
Reston, VA 22091
703-264-9435

**EPIC English Plus Information Clearinghouse**
220 Eye Street, NE, Suite 220
Washington, D.C. 20002
202-544-0004

**Intercultural Development Research Association**
5835 Callaghan Road, Suite 350
San Antonio, TX 78228
512-684-8180

**International Association of Applied Linguistics (AILA)**
602 Ballantine Hall
Indiana University
Bloomington, IN 47407
812-355-0097

**JNCL-NCLIS Joint National Committee for Languages/National Council for Languages and International Studies**
300 Eye Street, NW, Suite 211
Washington, D.C. 20002
202-546-7855

**Modern Language Association (MLA)**
10 Astor Place
New York, NY 10003
212-475-9500

**National Association for Bilingual Education (NABE)**
810 First Street, NE, Third Floor #300
Washington, D.C. 20002
202-289-1380

**National Center for Language Education and Research (CLEAR)**
1000 Glendon Avenue, Suite 1740
Los Angeles, CA 90024
213-206-1486

**National Center for Research on Cultural Diversity and Second Language Learning**
University of California
Santa Cruz, CA 95064
408-459-4899

**National Clearinghouse for Bilingual Education (NCBE)**
1118 22nd Street, NW
Washington, D.C. 20037
800-321-NCBE

**National Clearinghouse for Bilingual Education, Computerized Information System (NCBE CIS)**
1118 22nd Street, NW

Washington, D.C. 20037
800-321-NCBE
202-467-0867

**National Council of La Raza**
20 F Street, NW, 2nd Floor
Washington, D.C. 20001
202-628-9600

**National Council of Teachers of English (NCTE)**
1111 Kenyon Road
Urbana, IL 61801
217-328-3870

**National Institute for Multicultural Education (NIME)**
844 Grecian NW
Albuquerque, NM 87107
505-344-6898

**Network of Educators' Committees of Central America (NECCA)**
1118 22nd Street, NW
Washington, D.C. 20037
202-429-0137

**Office of Bilingual Education and Minority Languages Affairs**
U.S. Department of Education
330 C Street, NW, Room 5082
Washington, D.C. 20202
202-732-5063

**Teachers of English to Speakers of Other Languages (TESOL)**
1600 Cameron Street, Suite 300
Alexandria, VA 22314
703-836-0774

# Glossary

ABSTRACT NOUN.  An abstract noun names a quality or idea. Examples: *beauty, trust, fear, patience.*

ACCENT.  The relative stress, emphasis or degree of loudness placed on a syllable. Examples: a-ble, in-struct. Accent also refers to the pronunciation style associated with speakers of a region. Examples: *a French accent, a southern accent.*

ACHIEVEMENT TEST.  A standardized test that measures how much students know in a subject field; results are often reported in grade equivalent scores or as percentiles.

ACTION SERIES.  In language learning, a sequence of statements about actions being performed.

ACTIVE VOICE.  A verb is in the active voice when the subject is the doer or agent of the action. Example: *Marie baked the pie.*

ADJECTIVE.  A word that describes a noun or a pronoun, and tells what kind, how many, or which one. Examples: *lazy, beautiful, three, that.*

ADVERB.  An adverb describes a verb, an adjective, or another adverb by providing information about where, when, how, how much, or to what extent. Examples: *outside, later, seriously, few.*

AFFECTIVE.  Affective refers to feelings, emotions, or beliefs, as in an affective filter.

AFFECTIVE FILTER.  The unconscious act of changing, distorting, or blocking information as a reaction to its emotional or psychological content.

ALLOPHONE.  The variations of sounds associated with a single phoneme. Allophones are the result of the phoneme's juxtaposition to other phonemes. Allophones do not change meaning. Example: *the variation of the /p/ sound in pick/cup.*

ANALOGY.  A correspondence between two things based on a similar feature or application of a rule. In language learning, grammatical structures are often applied and practiced using analogy. Example: *set:setting::get: _____.*

APTITUDE TEST.  A test used to predict how well students will perform in a subject area; most are based on the presumption that certain underlying abilities or factors contribute to success in more than one field.

ARTICLE.  Articles, also called determiners, are adjectives that precede and identify nouns. A definite article (*the*) points to a particular item; an indefinite article (*a, an, some*) points to an entire class of items; a partitive article (*a few, some, a lot of, many, a little, much*) points to a portion of the class of items. Examples: *the ticket, a box, a few raisins.*

ARTICULATION.  The purposeful production of sounds by the vocal organs.

AUDIO-LINGUAL METHOD.  In language teaching, a method in which the student listens to the spoken message and then repeats it. This instructional process is also called the aural-oral method.

AUXILIARY VERB.  An auxiliary verb, also called a helping verb, is used with the main verb for verb forms that show tense and mood. Examples: *will go, has been crying, had gone.*

BACKWARD BUILD-UP.  A language teaching strategy in which a word or sentence is broken into components and reconstructed in a series of repetitions beginning with the end, then the next to the end plus the end, etc. This is particularly useful in practicing stress and intonation patterns. (See Right-to-left strings.)

BICULTURAL. Bicultural means identifying with and exhibiting the characteristics of two cultures.

BIDIALECTAL. Having the ability to speak and understand two dialects of a single language.

BILINGUAL. Having the ability to speak and understand two languages.

CHAINED DIALOGUE. In language teaching, chained dialogue is a practice exercise in which the first speaker makes a statement or asks a question, the second speaker responds to the first, the third speaker responds to the second, and so on.

CHORAL RESPONSE. A response made by a group speaking the same words in unison.

CLOZE TEST. A cloze test is based on the student's use of context clues to complete a word, sentence, or passage by supplying letters or words that have been deleted. As a test, it is used to judge comprehension; as an instructional method, it can be used to focus attention on discrete spelling or grammar items.

CLUSTER. A group of letters or sounds frequently occurring together. Example: *-ble, spr-*.

CODE. A system of symbols, letters, or words used to transmit meaning. Code also refers to the total language system of a community.

COGNATE. Cognates are words in different languages that have similar spellings and meanings. Example: *admiration/admiracion (English/Spanish)*.

COGNITIVE CODE THEORY. A theory of language acquisition that posits that language is governed by rules and is learned by repeated exposures to examples of the rules.

COLLECTIVE NOUN. A collective noun names a group or collection of people or things. Examples: *family, army, group, flock, band, herd*.

COMMON NOUN. A common noun names one of a class or group of persons, places, or things. Common nouns are not capitalized. Examples: *state, sea, building*.

COMPOUND NOUN. A compound noun is made up of two or more words. Examples: *seatbelt, brothers-in-law, sunshine*.

CONCRETE NOUN. A concrete noun can be perceived by one or more of the senses. Examples: *book, snow, steam, child*.

CONJUNCTION. A word that is used to join words, phrases, or clauses. Examples: *and, or, because, however, but*.

CONNOTATION. The connotation of a word or phrase is its meaning based on context or usage, not on the literal definition of the word or words.

CONSTITUENT. In language, a constituent is the smallest structural unit carrying meaning. Example: *town/s, carry/ing*.

CONTENT AREA VOCABULARY. The vocabulary associated with a particular subject of study. Example: *mathematics vocabulary, journalism vocabulary, political vocabulary*.

CONTENT WORDS. In language, content words are the words naming things, actions, and qualities.

CONTEXT. The factors surrounding the experience that help shape its meaning. Example: *The meaning of a test score depends on its context—a score of 5 on a test with a range of scores from 1 to 100 vs. a score of 5 on a test with a range of scores from 1 to 5.*

CONTINUANT.  A sound that can be extended or prolonged. Example: /m/, /s/.

CONTINUUM.  A sequence in a process or gradations of value where the parts of the continuum are arbitrarily divided.

CONTRASTIVE ANALYSIS.  In language, contrastive analysis is the comparison of the features of two or more languages. Frequently a contrastive analysis of the student's native language and the language being studied is used as an instructional tool.

CORRELATION.  A positive or negative relationship between two things, where change in one will result in a change in the other.

COUNTABLE NOUN.  A countable noun can be modified by a numeral and has both singular and plural forms. Examples: *one pillow, five pillows; one bed, two beds.*

CRITERION-REFERENCED TEST.  A test that determines whether the test taker has mastered a particular skill sufficiently by comparing the performance of the test taker to a fixed standard or criterion. Criterion-referenced tests are often used as placement or promotion tests.

CUE.  A stimulus used to elicit or provoke a response. Cues can be verbal or nonverbal. Examples: *a question cues an answer; raised eyebrows cue an explanation.*

CULTURAL PLURALISM.  Cultural pluralism refers to two or more ethnic groups coexisting in a community.

CULTURE.  The accumulated history, language, customs, values, art, literature, and achievements of a group.

DECODE.  To get meaning from language or other symbols.

DEMONSTRATIVE PRONOUN.  A demonstrative pronoun identifies or points out a noun. Examples: *that, this, these, those, such.*

DENOTATION.  The literal meaning or dictionary definition of a word.

DENTAL.  A dental sound is produced using the teeth in articulation.

DERIVED.  In language learning, a derived word, phrase, or sentence is produced by applying a transformation rule to the basic word, phrase or sentence. Example: *biker, biking, bikes are derived from the basic word bike.*

DESCRIPTIVE ADJECTIVE.  A descriptive adjective tells some quality of the noun. Examples: *pretty girl, soft pillow.*

DETERMINER.  In grammar, a determiner is a word that signals a noun. Examples: *articles (a, the); demonstrative adjectives (these, that); partitives (some, each).*

DIAGNOSTIC TEST.  A test that determines a student's strengths and weaknesses in a subject. Diagnostic test results answer the question, "Which of these skills or understandings does the student possess?"

DIALECT.  A variant of a language spoken by people of a particular geographic region.

DIPHTHONG.  A sound created by combining two vowel sounds. Example: *long i.*

ENCODE.  To represent something in an agreed form using a pattern or system of representation that has meaning for others. Examples: *American Sign Language, Morse Code, English.*

EQUIVALENT. A word or expression that conveys the same meaning as another word or expression.

FADE. In language teaching, fade means to gradually withdraw cues or gradually reduce volume.

FALSE COGNATE. False cognates are words in different languages that have similar spellings but have very different meanings.

FORMULA. In language learning, a formula is a common expression of greeting, leave-taking, etc., that is used almost automatically. Examples: *See you later. God bless you. How do you do?*

FRAME. In language learning, a frame refers to an exercise in which students insert, in various positions or slots in the sentence, a word or words that will form a semantically and grammatically correct sentence.

FRICATIVE. (See Continuant.)

FUNCTION WORDS. Words that convey little meaning by themselves but are used to show relationships among content words. Examples: *articles, prepositions, conjunctions.*

GIST. Gist refers to the main ideas of any spoken or written communication.

GRADE EQUIVALENT SCORE. A statistically estimated grade level for which a test score is the presumed average score. Example: *a student achieving a grade equivalent score of 6.5 performed as well on the test as the average student midway through sixth grade would have performed on that test.*

IDIOM. A word or expression whose meaning is not derived from the literal meaning of the word or words.

INCREMENTAL LEARNING. Incremental learning builds upon previously learned information a little at a time.

INDEFINITE PRONOUN. An indefinite pronoun refers to a general, not specific, person or thing. Examples: *one, some, no one, anybody, several, both, many, few, all.*

INFLECTION. The change in pitch in spoken language. Inflection also refers to the form of a word used to indicate number, tense, mood, voice, or person.

INTERJECTION. A word that is used alone to express strong emotion. Examples: *Oh! Congratulations! Damn! Bravo!*

INTERROGATIVE PRONOUN. An interrogative pronoun is used to ask a question. Examples: *who, what, whom, whose, which.*

INTONATION. The relative levels of pitch in a sentence; the variation of the four usual speech pitches (below normal, normal, somewhat above normal, very much above normal).

INTRANSITIVE VERB. An intransitive verb does not have an object. Example: *The baby cried.*

IRREGULAR VERB. An irregular verb does not form its past tense and past participle by adding -d or -ed to the verb base. The past and past participle forms do not follow a pattern. Examples: *go, went, gone; see, saw, seen.*

JUNCTURE. The separation or space between sounds that demark the words. Examples: *I/scream:ice/cream; solo:so/low.*

KERNAL SENTENCE. The basic sentence containing a noun phrase and a verb phrase.

KINESICS. Kinesics refers to nonverbal communication, including gestures, facial expressions, stance, etc.

LABIAL. A labial sound uses the lips in its articulation.

LEXICON. The words of the language.

LIMITING ADJECTIVE. A limiting adjective narrows the noun or concept being told about; possessive adjectives, demonstrative adjectives, and interrogative adjectives limit nouns. Examples: *his sweater, several chairs, whose sandwich.*

LINGUISTICS. The descriptive, analytic science of languages.

LINKING VERB. A linking verb connects the subject and complement that describes or relates back to the subject. Examples: *José is president. The old man seems tired.*

LOCAL NORMS. Local norms are performance standards established using school or district results on a test or other performance indicator.

MARKER. A word or word part that identifies the grammatical function of a word. Example: *the words "a" and "the" are noun markers.*

MASS NOUN. (See noncountable noun.)

MEAN. The arithmetic average of a group of scores.

MEDIAN. The middle score in a group of scores.

MIMICRY. In language learning, mimicry is the repetition of a speech model for the purpose of memorizing it.

MINIMAL PAIR. A minimal pair consists of two words that differ by one sound. Examples: *beg/peg, spool/spell, kid/kit.*

MODAL AUXILIARY VERB. A modal auxiliary verb indicates possibility, need, ability, willingness, or obligation. Modals include can, could, should, may, might, must, ought, shall, will, would. Examples: *You may stay out late. I ought to call home.*

MODAL SCORE. The score most frequently earned by the test takers.

MORPHEME. The smallest unit of speech that conveys meaning. Bound morphemes cannot stand alone (-ed designates past tense); free morphemes can stand alone (toy).

NASAL. A nasal sound requires the flow of air through the nose for articulation.

NATIONAL NORMS. Performance standards established by administering the test or other performance indicator to a group of people representative of the national population.

NATURAL ORDER HYPOTHESIS. The natural order hypothesis is the assumption that language elements are learned in a reasonably fixed order by all language groups.

NONCOUNTABLE NOUN. A noncountable noun refers to something that cannot be counted. Examples: *justice, trouble, air, beer, coffee, gold, juice, tea, water, paper, electricity, work.*

NORM-REFERENCED TEST. A test that compares the performance of the test taker to the performance of similar individuals who have previously taken the test (See Norming Population.)

NORMAL DISTRIBUTION. A statistical distribution of performance scores in which the mean, mode, and median scores are the same and the proportion of performance scores declines as performance moves away from the mean.

NORMING POPULATION. The group of people used to establish performance standards for age or grade levels on a test or other performance indicator. The composition of the norming population must be similar to that of the population of interest for a standardized test to be appropriate.

NOUN. A noun names or points out a person, place, thing, or idea. It can act or be acted upon. Examples: *teacher, home, bike, democracy.*

PASSIVE VOICE. A verb is in the passive voice when the subject is the receiver of the action. Example: *The pie was baked by Marie.*

PATTERNED PRACTICE. In language learning, patterned practice is the repetition of structured sentence patterns and includes the substitution of elements in the sentence and modifications to other parts of the sentence to retain correct syntax. Example: *I have a rose. I have two roses.*

PERCENTILE RANK. The comparison of the test taker's score with the scores of others and reported as the percentage of all test takers who scored equal to or below the test taker's score. Example: *a percentile rank of 94 means the test taker's score was equal to or above the score of 94 percent of the total group of test takers.*

PERSONAL PRONOUN. A personal pronoun refers to one or more individuals or things. Personal pronouns have three cases: nominative (examples: *I, he, we*), possessive (examples: *my, his, our*), and objective (examples: *me, him, us*).

PHONEMES. The sounds of a language.

PHONEMICS. The study of the sounds of a language.

PHONETICS. The study of the sounds of speech and their production.

PHONICS. The study of sound/spelling correspondences in a language.

PITCH. The lowness or highness of a sound or tone.

PLOSIVE. A plosive sound requires a burst of air through the lips for articulation.

POSSESSIVE PRONOUN. A personal pronoun that shows ownership when used with a noun. Examples: *my hat, our tickets, their dog.*

PREPOSITION. A word that is used to show the relationship of a noun or pronoun to another word. Examples: *to, on, across, below, of, at, from.*

PROFICIENCY TEST. A standardized test in which the performance of the student is compared with a standard or criterion used to describe a condition of proficiency or competence. (See Criterion-Referenced Test.)

PROMPT. A stimulus used to elicit a response. (See Cue.)

PRONOUN. A pronoun is used in place of a noun. There are personal, interrogative, relative, indefinite, demonstrative, and reflexive pronouns. Examples: *it, my, I, them, who, that.*

PROPER ADJECTIVE. A proper adjective is derived from a proper noun. Always capitalize a proper adjective. Examples: *Italian bread, Irish coffee.*

PROPER NOUN. A proper noun names a specific person, place, or thing. Always capitalize a proper noun. Examples: *Jennifer, Texas, North Sea, Eiffel Tower, Central Park.*

RAW SCORE. The number of items a test taker gets correct on a test. Raw scores have little meaning without a point of reference. Example: *a raw score of 19 is very good if the highest possible score is 20; it is poor if the highest possible score is 200.*

REDUNDANCY.   In language, redundancy is the presence of multiple signals of linguistic information. Example: *The actress opened her suitcase.* "-ess" and "her" indicate the subject is female.

REFERENT.   A referent is the actual thing, action, quality, or idea to which a word refers.

REFLEXIVE PRONOUN.   A reflexive pronoun refers to a noun and provides emphasis or shows distinction from others; reflexive pronouns are formed with the suffixes -self and -selves. Examples: *Mary told me herself. The boys fixed the car by themselves.*

REGISTER.   A systematic variation, including select vocabulary, sentence structure and tone, associated with different communication environments. Example: *different registers are used for ceremonial language vs. dialogue among friends; explanations to adults vs. explanations to young children.*

REGULAR VERB.   A regular verb forms its past tense and past participle by adding the suffix -d or -ed to the verb base. Examples: *look, looked, looked; thank, thanked, thanked.*

REJOINDER.   A response to a reply.

RELATIVE PRONOUN.   A relative pronoun relates groups of words to nouns or other pronouns. Examples: *who, which, that.*

RELIABILITY.   In assessment, reliability is a measure of the extent to which a test would yield consistent results if given under the same circumstances an unlimited number of times. The higher the reliability coefficient of a test, the more likely the scores of the test takers are reasonable indicators of their performance on that test.

RHYTHM.   The regular pattern in speech sequences caused by the position of accented and unaccented syllables.

RIGHT-TO-LEFT STRINGS.   Right-to-left strings are used to teach intonation patterns in oral language. In a right-to-left string, the last sound or word is pronounced first, then the next to last plus last, and so on, until the entire word or sentence is constructed from right to left and pronounced. Example: *ball. the ball. hit the ball. Jill hit the ball.*

SEGMENTAL PHONEMES.   Vowels and consonants are segmental phonemes.

SEMANTICS.   The study of word meanings and communication.

SLOT.   In language study, a slot is the position of a word or group of words in a sentence. (See Frame.)

STANDARDIZED TEST.   A standardized test is one for which norms or standards have been established using a select population of test takers under set conditions.

STANINE SCORE.   A score from 1 to 9 assigned to a raw score for performance on a test or other performance indicator. Stanine scores have a mean of 5 and a standard deviation of 2.

STOP.   In linguistics, a stop is a consonant that requires a stoppage of breath to articulate. Examples: /p/, /t/.

STRESS.   (See Accent and Rhythm.)

STRING.   In language teaching, a string is a sequence of letters or words.

STRUCTURE.   In language teaching, structure refers to the grammatical forms of a language.

SUPRASEGMENTAL PHONEMES. Suprasegmental phonemes refer to language features such as pitch, stress, and juncture added to the sounds of vowels or consonants.

SYNTAX. The acceptable pattern of the parts of speech in a language; common grammatical patterns.

TAGMENE. The word and the position in the sentence that it fills. (See Frame, Slot.)

TENSE. The form that indicates the relative position in time of the action or state of being referred to in the sentence. The three simple tenses are present, past, and future. The progressive form of the tenses is used to show continuing action.

TRANSFER. In language learning, transfer is the person's use of knowledge of his or her native language in the study of a new language.

TRANSITIVE VERB. A transitive verb relates an action that has an object. Example: *Ellen baked the bread.*

VALIDITY. In assessment, validity is the measure of the extent to which a test measures what it purports to measure.

VERB. A word that shows a physical or mental action, or the state of being of a subject. Examples: *sit, think, appear, know.*

VOICED. A voiced sound is produced with the vocal cords vibrating. Examples: the*se, *butter.*

VOICELESS. A voiceless sound is produced without the vocal cords vibrating. Examples: th*in, *pat.*